# Database-Driven Web Development

# Learn to Operate at a Professional Level with PERL and MySQL

## Second Edition

Thomas Valentine

apress®

*Database-Driven Web Development: Learn to Operate at a Professional Level with PERL and MySQL, Second Edition*

Thomas Valentine
Selkirk, MB, Canada

ISBN-13 (pbk): 978-1-4842-9791-9        ISBN-13 (electronic): 978-1-4842-9792-6
https://doi.org/10.1007/978-1-4842-9792-6

Copyright © 2023 by Thomas Valentine

Managing Director, Apress Media LLC: Welmoed Spahr
Acquisitions Editor: Divya Modi
Development Editor: James Markham
Editorial Assistant: Divya Modi

Cover designed by eStudioCalamar

Cover image by Freepik (www.freepik.com)

Distributed to the book trade worldwide by Springer Science+Business Media New York, 1 New York Plaza, Suite 4600, New York, NY 10004-1562, USA. Phone 1-800-SPRINGER, fax (201) 348-4505, e-mail orders-ny@springer-sbm.com, or visit www.springeronline.com. Apress Media, LLC is a California LLC and the sole member (owner) is Springer Science + Business Media Finance Inc (SSBM Finance Inc). SSBM Finance Inc is a **Delaware** corporation.

For information on translations, please e-mail booktranslations@springernature.com; for reprint, paperback, or audio rights, please e-mail bookpermissions@springernature.com.

Apress titles may be purchased in bulk for academic, corporate, or promotional use. eBook versions and licenses are also available for most titles. For more information, reference our Print and eBook Bulk Sales web page at http://www.apress.com/bulk-sales.

Any source code or other supplementary material referenced by the author in this book is available to readers on GitHub (github.com/apress). For more detailed information, please visit https://www.apress.com/gp/services/source-code.

Paper in this product is recyclable

# Table of Contents

# About the Author

**Thomas Valentine** has 20 years of experience as both a professional web developer and writer. He is a LAMP, Perl, PHP, and MySQL web developer, programmer, and expert. He writes for various magazines and websites and has been a technical consultant for large-scale, database-driven websites such as FedEx.ca and Texas Instruments (ti.com).

# About the Technical Reviewer

**Kenneth Fukizi** is a software engineer, architect, and consultant with experience in coding on different platforms internationally. Prior to dedicated software development, he worked as a lecturer and was then head of IT at different organizations. He has domain experience working with technology for companies mainly in the financial sector. When he's not working, he likes reading up on emerging technologies and strives to be an active member of the software community.

Kenneth currently leads a community of African developers, through a startup company called AfrikanCoder.

# CHAPTER 1

# Database-Driven Web Development Fundamentals

The database was first created by software engineers at North American Rockwell in the mid-1970s. They were previously using static files to catalogue the work they were producing. They began to notice that efforts were being duplicated, as a project such as the designing of an Apollo-era rocket generates hundreds of thousands of different parts. Each part was given a static file. Keeping track of these hundreds of thousands of parts was a nightmare before the relational database was put into practice. With it, they were able to find the duplicated efforts and eliminate them.

We'll begin this chapter by reviewing the fundamentals of database-driven websites before moving on to the pros and cons of web hosting, delving into the options that are available. You'll see how the modern database fits into the process of using three different servers (the Perl, Apache, and MySQL servers) to generate a web page. These three servers are what we'll be learning to use together in this book. Read on, it's going to be fun!

## The Evolution of the Database-Driven Approach

During the infancy of the Internet, databases weren't used with websites. All pages were static HTML pages. Today, they'd be pretty boring sites to surf, as we've all become accustomed to the modern database-driven website.

The world caught on to the idea that databases were the more efficient way to go, eventually leading to our database-driven world. All of our worldly services from banking to social networks now use a database of some flavor.

1

© Thomas Valentine 2023
T. Valentine, *Database-Driven Web Development*, https://doi.org/10.1007/978-1-4842-9792-6_1

Of particular note is the Internet. Databases are widely used to serve the pages that we all look at every day. They integrate seamlessly into a web page and have changed the world we live in. Databases are here to stay, so it is of paramount importance that you know a thing or two about them.

Since the database runs on a server, there has to be a way to access these databases. There are many different ways to do this, as there are many different languages used in modern computing. We'll be concentrating on the interactions between the MySQL database and the Perl scripting language.

Perl has great capabilities when it comes to interacting with databases. It is a powerful language that has been around for decades. It is a mature technology and is best suited to working with text. Perl stands for Practical Exporting and Reporting Language and was first used to manipulate text within common static text files. Since the languages we use in web development are textually based, Perl is the way to go when dealing with large textual documents (e.g., HTML markup).

Coupled with a database, Perl is a powerful and capable engine to power the modern website. Perl usually runs on the same server or at least the same network that the database runs on. This allows for fast and efficient interactions comprised of large blocks of textual data, such as the HTML code used in every page on the Internet today.

Databases are evolving to fill the need for newer, faster, and more powerful websites. It is common for one website to use many databases to serve its web pages. This scalable ability is the cornerstone of today's website. As the site grows, more databases are required to run the website. Parceling your website data from one or two databases into, say, a dozen allows you to access these databases from different parts of the website in a timely fashion under a heavy user load.

# How to Spot a Database-Driven Website

Most people just take it for granted that their web page will just load with the information they expect to be there. As a developer, you need to know how to spot a database-driven website. There are a few ways you can do this. We'll examine the different ways to spot one and to know, in general, what database is being used, in what way, and why.

# The Website Address (URL)

The first, and perhaps easiest, method to use to spot a database-driven website is the URL in the address bar of the browser. If you were to look at a web page that is a static HTML page, you would see an address that ends in a file name with the .html file extension. Examine the following example:

`http://www.domain.com/index.html`

You can see the constituent parts of the web address clearly: the address starts with the standard `http://www.domain.com` and ends with the file named index.html.

Most websites use index.html as the default starting point of their website. It is the main page that the Apache web server sees as the base file of any given website, although it is entirely possible to use a different file name as the starting point of your website. Configuring your web server is tackled in a coming chapter of this book.

The .html extension tells you that the page is a static HTML page. There is nothing to the right of the address bar, so it is a good bet that a database isn't being used at all on that website.

When you use Perl to present a database-driven page, the file extension is either .cgi or .pl. If there's a database being used, a question mark will be displayed after the file name extension. What follows the question mark is unique to each website. Examine the following URL:

`http://www.domain.com/thisfile.cgi?id=1234`

You can see the basic constituent parts of a URL, including a Perl script named thisfile with the extension .cgi. Then comes a question mark followed by the "id=1234" statement. This is a good indicator that a database is being used. There may be many different statements after the question mark, each separated with an ampersand (&), as follows:

`http://www.domain.com/thisfile.cgi?id=1234&id2=5678`

You can see now that the URL shows two different statements called parameters. These parameters show that two sets of data within the parameters are being passed to the server. While it is possible that a database isn't being used with these parameters, it is very uncommon to see more than one parameter that is being used without a database being in the loop somewhere.

# Differing Content Areas

You can also see that a database is being used by clicking a few links and noticing that one page looks very much like the previous, but with different content being displayed in the main content areas. This is because a database-driven site commonly uses templates to present their data. By template I mean a set of markup (such as HTML) that is used to present the top and bottom and sides of the page, for example. The only part of the page that changes is, say, the center of the page. This is the database-generated content.

Another easy way to spot a database-driven site is by paying attention to the advertising banners and buttons. If they change with every page or even if you refresh the page, the advertisement changes. This can't be done without using a database on some level.

When working with Perl and a database, you'll notice that a dialog box will be presented by the browser asking if you'd like to "repost form data." This is because you've just finished posting data to a database and have clicked the "Back" button on your browser. The Perl script that posted the information is being run again, making the same database entry you just made again.

On the Perl scripts that don't interact with a database, you won't see the "repost form data" dialog box. As we progress through the chapters of this book, you'll notice that this happens quite often. One of the only ways around this is to provide, within the Perl script, an easy-to-recognize link that takes you back to the previous page without reposting the form data and duplicating the database entry.

Reposting the form data can be detrimental to your site, as it duplicates the data within your database. While the Perl script being rerun may be something as simple as counting a page hit, it may be something as complicated as uploading a dozen images to your server – you'll see that the 12 images are duplicated on your server.

# Adding Search Features

One surefire way of detecting that a website is using a database is if the site offers up search features. While it is possible to search a website without using a database, this is costly in terms of server resources and isn't done very often. Searching through dozens or even hundreds of static HTML files would take an inordinate amount of time and server resources.

Searching for content via a database, however, is exactly what the database was created for. MySQL is great for doing this, as it is a relational database. We'll discover more on the term "relational database" in a different section of this chapter.

Search features are a common sight on most database-driven websites. MySQL, along with Perl, can incorporate some very powerful search features into your site. The project we'll be working on in later chapters of this book includes a search feature that finds users and posts based on a word or phrase entered into a search field by you, the user.

# Username and Password Considerations

One definite and easy way to spot that you're using a database is if you have to sign in with a username and password. While there is a way to use a username and password without using a database, this method doesn't involve a true database.

When supplying a username and password, the script tells the database to first look for the username. Once the username is found, the password is retrieved. Once retrieved, if the password on file mirrors the password provided, the user is logged in. From there on in, a database is most commonly used to present the page to the user, most of the time based on some aspect of the user's personal information.

# Protect a Directory with .htaccess Files

The only way to use a username and password without using a traditional database is with an older method of recognizing a user. This older method is by using an .htaccess file. Within this file is a name/value pair that contains the username and password. An .htaccess file is simply a text file with commands and data within it.

Once the username and password are verified, the directory directly below where the .htaccess file resides on your server will be able to be accessed by that particular user. This check is made by the Apache web server, not Perl nor a database.

While this works fine in some cases, you are limited to about 100 users. After the 100-user limit has been reached, it will take an inordinate amount of time to verify the username and password. This is because the supplied username and password must be verified by comparing both pieces of data to the 100 different name/value pairs within the simple .htaccess file.

While the operation of simple user verification is the base operation of an .htaccess file, it should be known that the Apache web server allows you to include special commands that limit or change the conditions of each page covered by that .htaccess file.

If you were a web master, in installing and configuring the Apache web server, you will have to make a certain set of changes in a configuration file known as httpd.conf. Within this file is all of the information the Apache web server requires to successfully serve a web page from that server. Most of these commands, such as for allowing user access, can be put into the .htaccess file. This handy functionality is why the .htaccess file is still being used on the Internet today.

# Where and When to Use a Database

You would normally use a database if you have a need to present a certain web page to your users that has as its main point of interest content that is changeable and fluid – a page that differs according to each user such as a user profile page, for example.

Using a database gives you the flexibility to present to your users dynamic content. By dynamic, it is meant data that changes, usually according to user action. The user that generated the data a user is looking at may not be the current user – since there is the potential to have thousands or even millions of users on one website, looking at data generated by a different user is commonplace.

If you see that you have a need to employ features such as displaying individual user information, search features, or are working with HTML forms in any number, you should be using a database.

While working with a database on the Internet, you'll be able to easily see where and how a database is being used within each site that you visit. You'll get an idea of the flexibility and power that a database-driven website can accomplish. Through the use of simple markup code such as HTML, you'll see that a database can extend the creative reach that is possible.

# Web Hosting Fundamentals

So you have an idea for a website and wish to pursue it and make it real. One of the first things you'll have to consider is who your web hosting company is going to be.

In a nutshell, there are three options for web hosting – the shared plan, the VPS (Virtual Private Server) plan, and the dedicated server plan – and each has its own pros and cons. We will look at each one in the remainder of the chapter.

# The Shared Server

Shared server plans are just what you think they are – you share your server with many different websites. This plan is great for developing your website in its infant stage. You would normally start out with the shared plan in order to develop your website into a finished product. It is the cheapest option that still gives a good amount of functionality, although it usually isn't the option to stay with if you plan on having a large amount of users. It should be noted that there are two ways your shared server will be addressed: name based or IP based. A name-based server address is the way we humans usually understand `www.domain.com`, for example. The other naming convention, IP based, is a numeric form of addressing that uses an "octet" of numbers. IP stands for Internet Protocol, that is, four groups of three numbers separated by a period:

127.34.56.124

The IP address as seen in the preceding example is a valid IP address. It contains four numbers separated by dots. These numbers are the base addressing system on the Internet. In order to match these numbers with words that us humans understand, we would have to use a DNS server. DNS stands for Domain Name Server.

Shared hosting plans usually have all of the functionality you'll need to get your website from nothing to a fully functioning Internet offering. However, there are a few things you have to know of before you sign the contract and pay the company for space on one of its servers.

Web hosting companies only allow a certain amount of resources for your site when using a shared server plan. Resources are things like disk space, a percentage of processor usage, and a limit on bandwidth that can be used, usually measured within a 30-day period.

Some limit the amount of MySQL databases you are able to create and use. You should ask your web host if your MySQL databases are on the same server you're using or accessed via the local network on a server dedicated to running MySQL databases. This is important because in order to use the database, you'll have to know whether to use a web address as the location if the database is on a dedicated server or "localhost" if the database resides on the same server the rest of your website is stored on. This addressing will be reflected in every Perl script that uses the database, so knowing this is important.

Since the primary scripting language of this book is Perl, it is important that you ask the web hosting company if they allow you to install more Perl modules that don't come with the standard Perl distribution, such as DBI.pm. In later chapters of this book, you will also need to use size.pm and resize.pm. size.pm and resize.pm are Perl modules that are used to return the size of an image (size.pm) and resize the image (resize.pm). More on those two Perl modules in a later chapter.

You should also ask your web host where the Perl executables are located. This piece of information is the one line of code at the very top of every Perl script, known as the "shebang." If the script can't find the Perl executables, the script won't run. The most common location of Perl is as follows:

```
#!/usr/bin/perl
```

I have encountered web hosting companies that list every recent version of Perl as the shebang, giving you the option of what version to use. Some companies use an unusual shebang. Look to the FAQ or support section of the web host's website for the location of Perl.

I have run into a web hosting company that doesn't offer Perl as a scripting language. Their excuse was that Perl is not scalable, which couldn't be further from the truth. Perl is infinitely scalable – you just have to know how to do it. Between the use of subdomains and files, you're able to spread an extremely complicated site over an entire array of servers.

# The VPS Server

The Virtual Private Server (VPS) plan is a step up from the shared plan in terms of server ability and customization. A VPS plan gives a guaranteed percentage of processor use, memory (RAM), and hard drive space. It closely emulates a dedicated server without the higher cost of a dedicated sever. Most plans also allocate more bandwidth per 30-day period than you would get with a shared server plan.

A VPS plan is one that emulates the functionality of a dedicated server. They're pricier than a shared plan, but the extra expense is usually worth the cost. Use a VPS server when you're in the final beta testing stage of your site's life cycle. Again, be careful about what is and isn't allowed on your VPS server. The VPS server is a good solution for low-traffic, low-bandwidth sites that require the functionality of a dedicated server without the added cost.

# The Dedicated Server

Dedicated plans are the costliest of the three common plan types and are also the most feature-rich, since it is usually only the one website on a single server. Some web hosting companies allow you to have more than one website on each dedicated server.

You would normally use a dedicated server after your site is complete and is already taking on users. They're the most expensive plan that a web hosting company provides, as yours is the only site using that server. Use a dedicated server when your traffic starts to bog down or you run low on hard drive space on your shared or VPS server.

Dedicated servers usually are offered on a sliding scale of functionality and capability. If you're going to lease a dedicated server, make sure it has hard drive redundancy, such as RAID 1. RAID stands for Redundant Array of Independent Disks.

The two most common flavors of RAID are RAID 1 and RAID 5. RAID 1 involves two separate hard drives that mirror each other's data. Only two hard drives are involved, with the idea being that if one hard drive fails, the data is still in a usable form on the other mirrored disk. This is the most common form of RAID.

RAID 5 is known as disk striping. Up to seven disks may be involved in storing your data. If one disk is lost, enough information remains on the other functioning hard drives to rebuild the data on the hard drive that had failed and was replaced.

# Email Options

Another basic service you should query your web host about is Linux's sendmail feature. While most people are familiar with Windows, it is rarely used on the Internet as a server. This is where Linux comes in. Linux is the prevalent server used to serve the web pages you see every day.

In order to send email via a script, you'll need sendmail to do it with. sendmail is a very basic email server that has been in use for decades. With it, you're able to send email on the fly according to scripted action.

You'll also want to ask about your online email client. There are many email clients to choose from, and all offer pretty much the same functions. What you're looking for, though, is a client that is stable and time tested. The most common email client is Horde, and it works very well. It is one of the oldest and most developed online email clients available. It is a mature technology. With it, you'll be able to retrieve and send email online from any computer with Internet service. The emails you receive are stored on your server and therefore are available from anywhere, should you memorize the address to the server.

## Secure Transactions

An important thing to ask about is whether or not you'll be able to use SSL (Secure Sockets Layer) in a portion of your website that collects payment information or information that is delicate in nature. Many web hosting companies only allow SSL on dedicated or VPS servers.

You can tell if a page is protected by SSL by looking to the address bar of the browser. Instead of having http:// at the beginning, the protocol should be https://. This shows you that a digital certificate is being used and your data is safe from prying eyes. Some websites don't limit the use of SSL to one section of the website in question – they use SSL to protect their entire website's data. While this is fine, it usually isn't warranted.

## Plesk or cPanel?

Most web hosting companies offer one of two different web applications to manage your server, those being Plesk or cPanel. They both cover pretty much the same functionality, with a few twists. They look slightly different but achieve the same thing. It is up to you to choose which server management application to use. Some like Plesk better, some cPanel. It is entirely up to you which application to use, as most web hosting companies give you the choice of the two most common server managers.

## Hard Drive Space and Data Transfer Limits

Another issue of concern is the amount of hard drive space you're going to be assigned. MySQL databases take up a lot of space, so you should have a shared plan with at least 5 GB of available hard drive space.

If you plan on uploading files, make sure you have space enough to sustain the site. If you're on a shared plan, go for the plan that offers the most hard drive space. When you use two-thirds of the space you've leased, it is time to make plans to upgrade your hosting solution. Your server manager (Plesk or cPanel) will tell you the amount of space used and what is remaining, both in easy-to-understand terms.

Most web hosting companies have restrictions on the amount of data transfer you're able to use within a 30-day period. Be sure to ask what the bandwidth limit for your account is and the fees you'll have to pay if your data transfer needs outweigh your bandwidth allocation.

# Resellers

Most web hosting companies allow reselling of their services via a third party. These resellers typically only offer shared web hosting at a very low price, such as $3.99 a month. They are exclusively a shared service provider and usually don't offer dedicated or VPS plans, so your upgrading options are limited.

While these resellers are fine during the infant stage of your site's life cycle, they can cause a bit of a problem if you have already gathered user data and have to move to a dedicated or VPS server. You'll have to find a way to get your user's data from the reseller's shared server to your primary web hosting company's dedicated or VPS server.

Using a web hosting company that isn't the primary service provider can sometimes cause lengthy delays in getting some changes made to your shared server as well. Your technical support request has to go through the reseller and then to the primary hosting company for a solution, then back to the reseller who in turn informs you of the outcome of your request. This amount of time can be lengthy, causing you to have to sit and wait for an outcome. So that's the shared server; let's move on to the VPS server.

# Installing Perl Modules

In working with Perl on the Internet, you'll eventually have the need to install more Perl modules to accomplish some task or other. As mentioned in the previous section, you would use Plesk or cPanel to do this. Both methods work fine and use either CPAN.bat or PPM. Exploring CPAN.bat and PPM is beyond the scope of this book.

# File Transfer Protocol (FTP) Clients

FTP clients are programs that allow you to access your files on your server remotely using FTP. With them, you are able to move around files on your server, create directories, and update your cgi scripts as you create and debug them.

There are many different FTP clients to choose from. The best by far, I've found, is a freeware application known as FileZilla. It has a connection manager that allows you to have a list of different websites to connect to as well as provides all of the functionality needed to work your website into a fully complete Internet offering.

## File Rights and Permissions

Every file on your server has a set of rights and permissions assigned to them. Some are assigned automatically, and some have to be assigned by you. Perl cgi scripts, once uploaded, lack the rights and permissions required to be run by your users via their browsers.

To assign the proper rights and permissions, look to your FTP client. There should be an easy way to change the rights and permissions of the file or files in question.

The Linux chmod command is what changes the permissions for a file. In FileZilla, simply highlight the file or files whose rights and permissions you need to change. Right-click the highlighted file or files and select Permissions. A dialog box will open with nine options to check. There is also a field where you can simply enter the proper rights and permissions code according to Linux's ranking system. To have a user run a cgi script on your server, enter "755" in this field (without quotes). You'll see that the dialog box updates the proper fields. Click OK and you've changed the file's rights and permissions to allow your users to execute the script via their browsers within your cgi-bin.

# Obtaining Your Path Statement with printenv.pl

One of the first things you need to know about your server's setup is the path statement. Within the path statement is the hierarchy of directories that extend from the root directory of your account to the working directories you'll be using, such as the cgi-bin directory that will hold all of your site's cgi scripts.

To obtain your path statement, it is required that you run a small but powerful script called printenv.pl. Simply upload the file and adjust its rights and permissions to chmod 755. Run the script in your browser and you'll be able to pick out the path statement. The following is code used in this small script:

```perl
print "Content-type: text/plain; charset=iso-8859-1\n\n";
foreach $var (sort(keys(%ENV))) {
    $val = $ENV{$var};
    $val =~ s|\n|\\n|g;
    $val =~ s|"|\\"|g;
    print "${var}=\"${val}\"\n";
}
```

This small piece of code tells you everything that is within the server's environment, including the path statement to many resources that will come in handy in later chapters of this book.

The path statements on a server are pointers to resources that are accessed directly from the operating system or the server in question. For example, a path statement in Windows can be set up to affect the Perl shebang. If you were to install Apache to c:\Apache, the shebang in your Perl script will be as follows:

```
C:\Apache\bin\perl
```

As you can see, the location allows for the server to find perl, but you may have to give the path to the perl.exe executable, as follows:

```
C:\Apache\bin\Perl\perl.exe
```

Giving the fully formed location to perl.exe is a security nightmare. Use it only if you don't want to set up an operating system's path statements from the control panel.

## Summary

In this chapter, we touched on the basic functionality of the various technologies we'll be using to create fully formed web pages. We discussed your web hosting options and how the three servers (Perl, MySQL, and Apache) are used together.

We touched on rights and permissions and basic knowledge that we will be building on in the chapters to come.

# CHAPTER 2

# Perl CGI and MySQL Essentials

The Perl Common Gateway Interface (CGI) module is a module capable of creating HTML markup code on the fly within your Perl script. It is mostly used as a means to catch the parameters of a page. While you could create entire pages with the methods included in the CGI module, it is a lengthy process and isn't very efficient. A simple print statement with your HTML markup as the printed material is a much more practical use of the CGI module.

In this chapter, we'll be exploring the Perl modules that will be used in the upcoming project. We'll also be using error control techniques and will introduce the methods used in the project to trap the errors in a manner that allows the script to continue running.

We'll then be exploring the syntax and use of Perl and the MySQL queries that we all will come across eventually and concentrate on retrieving information from the database, with a few exceptions for fun.

But first, let's quickly define CGI a bit further.

## CGI Primer

CGI is a combination of web standards that defines how information is exchanged between the web server and the script. CGI specifications are currently maintained by the NCSA that defines CGI as a standard for external gateway programs to interface with web servers such as HTTP servers. The CGI module was created in order to make available some of the higher forms of programming methods available in one compact and powerful source. With it, you're able to control forms, create page redirects, and access the Perl environment to retrieve things like the user's IP address.

15

© Thomas Valentine 2023
T. Valentine, *Database-Driven Web Development*, https://doi.org/10.1007/978-1-4842-9792-6_2

Through the methods of the CGI module, you will be able to create and control your Perl script's capabilities with only a few standard commands. I've found that working with HTML forms and CGI.pm is a good programming investment, as you're given a few options as to how the data submitted via the form will be handled.

# HTTP Methods

HTTP stands for Hypertext Transfer Protocol and is the base form of sending information over the Internet via your web page. An HTML form is the tool to interact with the server and send information from your web page to the CGI script via HTTP. There are a couple of ways to do this.

## The GET Method

The GET method of sending data from your web page to the server is perhaps the most common way of achieving this. The information within the form is sent to the server as part of the URL of the page. It is mostly used when you don't have a lot of data to be sent to the server. Examine the form element given in Listing 2-1.

*Listing 2-1.* Displaying the GET method of submitting FORM data

```
<form method="GET" action="/cgi-bin/perlscript.cgi" name="form1">
     <input type="TEXT" name="INPUT1"></input>
     <input TYPE"SUBMIT" name="SUBMIT1"></input>
</form>
```

You can see where the GET method is invoked within the HTML form element. You would use this if you have a small amount of information to be sent to the server to be acted upon and reported back. You wouldn't use the GET method when submitting a username and password to the server, as the username and password would be visible within the browser's address bar.

# The POST Method

The POST method of sending data to the server is for large blocks of information. The data is sent to the server in the body of the page submission. Only the URL of the script that the data is being sent to appears in the address bar of the browser. You would use the POST method if you're uploading an image, for example. Examine the example of using the POST method given in Listing 2-2.

***Listing 2-2.*** Applying the POST method of submitting FORM data

```
<form method="POST" action="/cgi-bin/perlscript.pl" enctype="multipart/
form-data" name="photo1">
     <input type="FILE" name="photo"></input>
     <input type"SUBMIT" value="SUBMIT PHOTO"></submit>
</form>
```

As you can see from the preceding example, the POST method was used to signify that the data is to be sent to the server within the body of the document. Notice also that an enctype attribute was used within the form element. This tells the server that a large block of data is being sent, in two forms – the data itself and the name of the data, in this case, the file name of the photo you're uploading. The input type is set to FILE. This tells the server that a file is being uploaded. When you are uploading a file, the browser opens a dialog box, within which are the folders and files on the hard drive of your computer. You would select a file and double-click it. It will then be made visible within the text box on the web page. Click the Submit button and the file will be uploaded via the Perl upload script named perlscript.pl.

# Running Perl CGI Programs

The Perl CGI.pm module is required to be installed within the Perl server for its libraries to be made available for use. The source files may be downloaded from CPAN.org in order for you to install the module. The Internet is a vast thing. The CPAN library contains hundreds of thousands of Perl modules in order to work in this vastness.

There are basically two ways that you can install a Perl module: CPAN.bat or the Perl Package Manager (PPM). Each is easy to use, requiring only the same knowledge required to configure Perl itself. By this, I mean simple path statements to resources on your computer such as, in this case, the location of Perl.

## CPAN.bat

CPAN.bat is an old-fashioned text-based batch file that runs on either Windows or Linux operating systems. It is easy to set up, requiring only the locations of Perl and a couple of other simple programs it may need in order to install the Perl modules.

Since it is a text-based program, you'll see a command-line utility box open once you double-click CPAN.bat. You can find CPAN.bat within the directories that make up Perl. It is in the same directory as the Perl executables, such as perl.exe itself.

Once configured, you simply enter the following command in order to install the CGI module:

```
install CGI
```

CPAN.bat will contact CPAN.org in order to fetch the executables required for the installation. A handy feature of CPAN.bat is its ability to also install any other Perl modules that may be required for the installing module. That is, CPAN.bat installs the other Perl modules that the CGI module will require to work properly.

## The Perl Package Manager

The Perl Package Manager is a bit easier to use than CPAN.bat. It has a GUI that is used primarily to display and manage all of the Perl modules you have installed.

While you can use CPAN.bat to see what modules you have installed, PPM displays the entire list as CPAN.bat only verifies the Perl module is installed according to your typing the name of the module in question. PPM is the better of the two at managing your Perl installation.

Installing a Perl module with the PPM is a breeze. A small command line is displayed. You enter the Perl module you'd like to install and it does so. I've found that some modules install better under PPM than CPAN.bat. The DBD.pm module for working with databases, for example, has problems installing via CPAN.bat, while it installs with a minimum of fuss with PPM. The in-depth use of both CPAN and PPM is beyond the scope of this book.

# Including the CGI Module in Your Script

In order for a Perl script to use any module ever made, it first must be declared with the use directive, as follows:

```
use CGI;
```

This line must be put at the top of the Perl script, just below the shebang. In order to start using the CGI module, you must first declare a new instance of the module:

```
$cgi = new CGI;
```

This generates a new instance of the CGI module and allows you to use the powerful methods contained within the CGI module as a whole.

# Manager Using the param() Method

One of the most oft-used methods made available by the CGI module is the param() method. It is used to catch the parameters sent to the Perl script from the HTML page the user is interacting with:

```
$param1 = $cgi->param('input1');
```

As you can see, catching a parameter with the CGI module is a simple affair. If you need more than one parameter caught, simply start a new param() method on the next line, as follows:

```
$param1 = $cgi->param('input1');
$param2 = $cgi->param('input2');
```

The second parameter is caught in exactly the same way as was the first. The only differences between the two are the Perl variable names and the parameter names. Simple.

# Obtaining Calling IP Address

As you'll see when we get into later chapters of this book, it is sometimes a necessity to know who is doing what on your website. In the project in later chapters, you'll be uploading photos to your server to be displayed as your avatar. Because this functionality can be maliciously attacked with illegal images or images that aren't suitable, it is of paramount importance that you know who is uploading the photo. The CGI module has prepared for this eventuality by including a means to retrieve the user's IP (Internet Protocol) address.

Every computer and server on the Internet has a unique IP address. This is needed because if you had two computers with the same IP address, the other computers on the Internet wouldn't know which one to send the information to.

The CGI module provides for this with the following simple statement:

```
$userip = $cgi->remote_host();
```

Using this simple-to-use line of code in your Perl script tells you the IP address of the person that has just interacted with your script. You need not limit this functionality to one upload script. Because it is so easy to use, you could record the user's IP address in every script that is being used and stuff it into your database.

## Making System Calls

Because CGI.pm doesn't do absolutely everything, you will soon find the need to use your server's operating system to retrieve certain pieces of information. The first thing that comes to mind is the date and time. CGI.pm can do a lot, but not time and date stamping. As you learned in a previous chapter, MySQL allows for time stamping, but that is only the time that the record was created in the database.

In order to make a system call, you would use the Perl backtick (`) operator. The following shows how to use the backtick operator to find the date:

```
$date = `date`;
```

As you can see, retrieving the exact date and time is a fairly simple and straightforward operation. Because the backtick operator allows for any system command to be executed, it is possible to work with files and directories via scripted action as well.

## Error Handling

In working with Perl, you'll have to include error handling within the structure of your script. By error handling, it is meant that unforeseen errors may occur that are either a pitfall of your script or as a product of malicious attacks by your users.

There are a few ways to handle errors in Perl, and we'll discuss all of them in this section. Before you can handle your errors, it is advisable that you first set your scripts up to report the error or errors properly. That is where the CGI::Carp module comes into play.

# CGI::Carp

This module is an invaluable tool for the developer. With it, the errors that are thrown by Perl are echoed to the browser for you to read there. If you weren't using CGI::Carp, your browser would display an "Error 500. A critical system error has occurred," which doesn't tell you much. You'd have to look in the Apache error log every time your script throws a fatal error. This can be very annoying and will certainly slow you down by a considerable amount of time.

The CGI::Carp module must be declared at the top of the script along with the other Perl modules the script will be using:

```
use CGI::Carp qw(fatalsToBrowser);
```

It may be entered in no particular order in the list of modules you're using. Used in this way, every error thrown will be sent to the browser. The error that has occurred is in plain language as well as the line of the Perl script and the Perl script name that the error occurred within is reported. You can then tell exactly what happened to cause the error and find a speedy solution to the problem.

# Where and When to Use Error Handling

Error handling can be a bit of a hit or miss thing. A fatal error may be thrown in a way and from a part of your script that you didn't think would cause problems. You'll learn where to use error handling as you debug your scripts.

I normally automatically include error handling on every database call. Even the slightest error is fatal when using MySQL. Most of the time the error is caused by the user using your script in a way that you didn't anticipate. Malicious users are the bane of every web developer as well.

There are a few ways to handle the errors that your scripts will throw. One is to wrap the Perl code in an eval statement or to redirect the user to a different custom error page.

# Handle Your Errors

The placement of your error handling is as important as the error handling itself. With database calls, the easiest way to handle your errors is after they've been thrown and redirect the user to a custom error page. I usually redirect to a custom error page that is written in HTML that logs the user out of the site, requiring them to log in again and hopefully not try the same action again. The following is the code to do this:

```
<meta http-equiv="refresh" content="0;url=/errors/error1.html">
```

This HTML code is given within the head of the document with the other meta elements. It tells the browser to fetch the page in the amount of seconds given. If you give a value of 0 for the time, the page redirects to the URL given upon page loading, not allowing the user to do anything but be redirected to the new error page.

# The External HTML Content Template

You'll eventually be at the point where you want to print your HTML content to the browser. There are a few ways you can do this, the easiest of which is to use a print statement for every line of HTML code that makes up your page. This is not recommended, as it is an inefficient means to print your page.

As you'll see in later chapters when we actually start displaying pages, there is an efficient means to accomplish a multiline printout to the browser – the external content template.

This template holds the HTML content that will be used to display the page. You may use as many templates as you wish. The templates are included in the script via a simple require statement:

```
require "content.pl";
```

Within content.pl is the HTML markup, along with variable and array names placed in strategic locations. The content.pl file is required near the end of the script, when all of the Perl script actions have been taken on the dynamic database-driven HTML code. Applying a template this way allows you to include a large amount of content in your page.

Within content.pl are two different variables and one array. The variables are
$topcontent and $bottomcontent, and the array is @contentarray. The content template
HTML tables end and start up again in a strategic way that allows the content between
them to be displayed inline and within the running markup code in order to make the
page appear as one coherent web page. For an example of this, examine Listing 2-3.

*Listing 2-3.*  An example of an external content template

```
<table cellpadding="0" cellspacing="0" border="0" align="center">
$topcontent
@contentarray
$bottomcontent
</table>
```

As you might surmise, $topcontent contains the markup that should appear on the
top of the database-generated content that is within @contentarray. $bottomcontent
closes up the markup so it fits with the static markup within content.pl.

# Printing Your Dynamic Content to the Browser

In order to print your generated and static content to the browser, the HTML markup
within content.pl is encased within one large variable, $htmlcontent. It is easy, then, to
print the dynamic content to the browser with just two easy-to-use commands:

```
print qq{Content-type: text/html\n\n};
print qq{$htmlcontent};
```

The first print statement tells the browser that the data being sent to it is of type text/
html, which is a fancier way of saying that what's coming is HTML markup. The second
print statement prints the huge $htmlcontent variable that contains both the static
markup from content.pl and the database-generated content that is within $topcontent,
@contentarray, and $bottomcontent.

# Perl and MySQL Basics

Perl and MySQL work together to achieve some very powerful procedures for the manipulation of your database data. Through the use of the Perl DBI module, it is possible to store and retrieve your database data in a very timely fashion. The DBI module is a great tool to work with, as it contains methods for just about any database machination you will run across.

We'll be exploring the syntax and use of Perl and the MySQL queries that we all will come across eventually. In this chapter, we'll concentrate on retrieving information from the database, with a few exceptions for fun.

In the examples that follow, every conceivable method of acquiring the data is presented. You'll see that the methods for retrieving the piece of data are simple and to the point. Once the data is retrieved, you may act upon it in any way you see fit. For simplicity's sake, the data will exist in the variables and arrays exactly as it appears in the database, always.

## Selecting One Database Item into One Variable

Retrieving one piece of information from a database is a straightforward operation, but there are some finer points that need to be addressed. First, what you need to do is decide if you're going to use the fetchrow() method or fetchrow_array() method. Since there is only one piece of information to be retrieved, the fetchrow() method will be used.

Note that it is entirely possible to use fetchrow_array() to catch the piece of data – you simply wouldn't because that is not what it was designed for. The fetchrow_array() method creates and loads an array into memory rather than a scalar variable. Since we're only taking out one piece of information from the database, it is not recommended that you use fetchrow_array() in this situation.

## Selecting a Piece of Data Using the Three-Step Method

Listing 2-4 shows how to define the query and place it in $query. You then prepare the query with the prepare() method and execute the query by calling the execute() method. You then catch the piece of data with the fetchrow() method and place it in $thisvariable.

***Listing 2-4.*** Applying the three-step method

```
$query = "SELECT id FROM this_table WHERE id = 12";
$sth = $dbh->prepare($query);
$sth->execute();
$thisvariable = $sth->fetchrow();
```

Note that a WHERE clause has been defined in the example. This is a great way
to select one or many similar pieces of information from the database. We'll explore
WHERE clauses in several upcoming examples. Stay tuned.

## Selecting a Piece of Data Using the Two-Step Method

With the following two-step method, we define the query within the prepare() method
and execute the query by calling execute(). In place of the $query variable from the
previous example, we send the textual database query as the argument to prepare(). We
then catch the piece of data with the fetchrow() method and place it in $thisvariable.

```
$sth = $dbh->prepare(SELECT id FROM this_table WHERE id = 12);
$sth->execute();
$thisvariable = $sth->fetchrow();
```

As you can probably glean from the example, this is a very basic construction.
For simple, clean code, you would only use simple MySQL queries with the two-step
method. The three-step method – where you simply have more room on that line – is
more suited to the multiline constructions we'll be using later in this book. Now we'll
explore the one-step method through the use of the do() method.

## Selecting a Piece of Data Using the One-Step Method

We used the do() method to define, prepare, and execute a database call, then catch the
piece of data with the fetchrow() method, and place it in $thisvariable. This is a great
method to use to clean up your code if you have many simple database queries in the
same script. With less to read, there is less confusion, and your code is cleaner in general.

```
$dbh->do(qq{SELECT id FROM this_table WHERE id = 12});
$thisvariable = $sth->fetchrow();
```

You would normally use the one-step do() method if you need to quickly perform a small amount of work. You wouldn't want to use the do() method with a foreach loop that is a million iterations long.

# Selecting Many Database Items into Many Variables

Since there will be a future need to select many pieces of information into many variables, the examples will show this. However, there are a few points to consider before continuing. This section of the book will delve into these points to remember and offer example tasks that reflect the functionality that we're shooting for.

There are two general functions that you may use to retrieve data from a database using the Perl DBI module. One is used for single pieces of data being pulled from the database. This is the fetchrow() method. It is used to retrieve single pieces of information from a database that will be stored either in one scalar variable or within one simple array. Since we'll be retrieving more than one piece of information, it is recommended that you use the fetchrow_array() method to achieve your database query.

The fetchrow_array() method is of a higher order than is the fetchrow() method, making the executions with this method very fast and very reliable. The simple constructions used with the fetchrow_array() method are effective and intuitive, which no doubt lends to the massive popularity of the Perl DBI module.

The database query itself must be of a sort that allows for more than one piece of data to be retrieved. Using a WHERE clause is the easiest and most straightforward way of accomplishing this. For example, if you were to use one definite value with your WHERE clause, you would only be able to retrieve one piece of data. Through the use of a WHERE clause that is designed to offer more than one result, the script is able to retrieve multiple values from multiple columns or rows, as the examples suggest. A simple > (greater than) operator achieves this very well, as you'll see in the coming examples.

The examples outline the constructions that can be used to retrieve many pieces of information and store them in several scalar variables. You can use an array in place of the variables, but this is not recommended. Keep your coding as simple as possible and you'll have the best results.

As always, the data retrieved should be presented in your variables and arrays as it exists in the database. This lends to a clean and concise database model and an easy-to-understand script. This is also a very easy-and-simple-to-implement approach to working with a database.

# Selecting Many Database Items into One Array

Let's start using arrays as the end product of our database queries. We'll begin with the simplest of constructions, pulling many pieces of information from the database and putting them in one array. Since there is only one piece of information to be pulled from the database at one time, the fetchrow() method will be used. The successive database data items are pushed onto an array to achieve the final result – an array that reflects your database columns exactly.

The example pulls many rows of data from one table and places the table data in one array. You may then access the data within the array by index numbers or loop through the entire array for one large list. Of note in the example tasks is the id >= 0, which tells MySQL to fetch all of the columns whose id value is greater than or equal to zero. This will essentially pull every row of the table and place the data in one array, which will be a perfect reflection of what you have in that one database column.

You wouldn't use fetchrow_array() because we are fetching only one column of the database table. Although we are fetching only one column, the columns will span across many rows. In this situation, the fetchrow_array() method is not needed. The fetchrow() method fits the need very well.

In the examples, it can be seen that every conceivable option for pulling data from the database is explored – the DBI module is a great piece of work to use. You can see from the example tasks that a very large amount of information can be fetched using the methods described. You may then act upon the data as you see fit. With a database call like this one, you are conceivably working with a very large amount of data. Constructing a list is a simple affair of looping through the index items with a foreach or while statement.

# Selecting Many Pieces of Information Using a WHERE Clause

WHERE clauses are wonderfully useful tools to use. They are easy to understand and use and make your database calls easy to implement. You can apply string or number type syntax. As you can see in Listing 2-5, mathematical operators may be used in your MySQL statement.

***Listing 2-5.*** Implementing a WHERE clause

```
$query = "SELECT col1 FROM this_table WHERE id >= 0";
$sth = $dbh->prepare($query);
$sth->execute();
while ($thisvalue = $sth->fetchrow()) {
    push @thisarray, $thisvalue;
}
```

We stated the database query and placed it in $query. We then called the prepare() method to prepare the $query for execution. The execute() method was used to execute the database call, and we used a while loop to iterate through the table columns, pushing the array for each iteration.

With Perl and MySQL, it is entirely possible to select a large amount of information in one database query. You eventually want to make some very large lists of information that reflect many columns and rows of the database. Like I said before, you want your arrays and variables to reflect the contents of your database.

Because the script makes multiple calls to the database, it is a necessity to keep things clear and simple by reflecting the database structure in your variables and arrays. For each row of the database, there is a corresponding set of arrays that represent the table columns. This simple yet effective method of reflecting the database structure in your variables and arrays is a good programming convention to stick to. It will make your more complicated future scripts much simpler to follow and will allow a much more complicated database model for future machinations.

The coming examples show how to put the data from many table rows in columns that reflect the structure of the database. You can see that the data retrieved is placed in three different arrays to be acted upon. The fetchrow_array() method of the DBI. pm module is used to perform the multicolumn query. Each column of the database is reflected in the arrays that follow, one array to each column. The rows are structured as the index items of each successive array.

# Selecting Many Items to Many Arrays

Selecting large pieces of varying data from the database can be a tricky thing for the uninitiated. This book, among other reasons, was written to dispel the questions that we all had about selecting many different pieces of information from your database.

The first thing to think about is the form you want your data to be in. That is, the arrangement of the arrays that we'll be using should reflect the database data perfectly. Each column will be selected into one array. Each row of that column will be an index item of the array. Using multiple arrays to represent multiple columns is a good programming convention to follow. It keeps the database data easy to understand and easier to act upon.

In the example that I've provided in Listing 2-5, the arrays are @col1, @col2, and @col3. They perfectly reflect the database data as it exists within the database. You can see that we used a simple array push to load the subsequent pieces of data into the three arrays.

You can see that through the use of a WHERE clause, we are able to select essentially every piece of data within those columns of the database. Using an operator such as >= (greater than or equal to) lets MySQL know exactly what pieces of information that you require. The id column is an AUTO_INCREMENT column.

You may order your query by the aforementioned AUTO_INCREMENT id column without selecting the id column into a variable or array – MySQL does the work for you. You don't even have to select the id column; just reference it in your query and MySQL will act accordingly. This has the benefit of keeping the number of variables or arrays at a manageable number and simplifies the script as a whole. The id column is present in every hypothetical table that we'll be using and is the primary key of the table.

The AUTO_INCREMENT id column is present in every table that we'll be using because it is such a handy way to refer to the contents of the table rows and columns. Using this method will ensure that you have the fastest and most capable queries possible with this combination of Perl, MySQL, and Apache. Consider the following:

```
$query = qq{SELECT col1, col2, col3 FROM $this_table WHERE id >= 0 ORDER BY
id DESC};
$sth = $dbh->prepare($query);
$sth->execute();
while (@this_data = $sth->fetchrow_array()) {
    push @col1, $this_data[0];
    push @col2, $this_data[1];
    push @col3, $this_data[2];
};
```

We constructed a query; in this case, the query is for three items: col1, col2, and col3. We prepare the query using the DBI.pm prepare() method. This reviews the query for syntactical correctness. We then execute the query using execute(). This sends the query to the database. Then we gathered the data using the DBI.pm fetchrow_array() method. The data is now contained in @col1, @col2, and @col3 and matches the database columns and rows exactly.

We used fetchrow_array() because we wanted more than one piece of information to be pulled from the database. For each iteration of the while statement, we gathered the data into the @this_data array. The data is then pushed into @col1, @col2, and @col3 using a simple push statement. The while statement then loops again, and a new set of data is pushed on @this_data, which is then pushed onto the three column arrays, and the process repeats until there is no more data to be retrieved from the database.

A few words should be given to system resources. Using such a powerful construction can potentially lead to an overwhelmed server. This is because of the massive amount of data that can be fetched into the three column arrays in our example. A good convention to follow regarding your data is related to the amount of RAM your server has available. On most systems, you may check the average amount of memory available using various programs. We won't get into the workings of such a program. What we need to know right now is the amount of free RAM you have on your server. Simply don't fetch more data than the amount of memory you have.

# Inserting Many Database Items from One Array

Using an array to insert your database items is a bit complicated but is still a fairly simple task. There are just a few things that you would have to consider while using this approach. This section will explain them.

Using a $count that increments with every iteration of the loop, it is possible to dynamically insert as many rows as you have a need for. Your limit is your resources, so a few words must be given to system resources. Because this method of inserting table rows is a very powerful one, it is possible to overwhelm your server by using an array that contains more data than can be handled successfully and in a timely fashion by the server. You wouldn't use a construction such as this to insert thousands of table rows with each piece of data having many kilobytes of information. The resulting operation, while still safe, might leave you with an overwhelmed server.

While it is possible to use a while loop in your constructions to achieve the same result, the efficiency and simplicity of the foreach loop with a $count variable make it a better choice. There is less to do with a foreach loop, since all we're doing is iterating through the array's index items and incrementing a count. The foreach loop automatically loops through the entire array and stops when it has reached the end of the array given as the argument.

With a while statement, you would have to have a test be performed to see if the $count matches the number of index items in the array. This slows things down, just a bit. However, if you know beforehand the number of items in the array, by all means use a while statement. Keep in mind this is only if you previously know the length of the array to be used.

# Using a foreach Loop to Insert from an Array

You can see from the example how looping through the array's index items is an easy thing with Perl. The $count variable keeps track of the index items for you so the database column exactly reflects the contents of @this_column. With each iteration of @this_column, the value of $this_column[$count] changed and was loaded into the database. We used a simple one-column MySQL statement to accomplish our task (Listing 2-6).

***Listing 2-6.*** Using a foreach loop to INSERT from an array

```
$count = "0";
foreach (@this_column) {
$query = qq{INSERT INTO this_table (col1)
    VALUES
       ('$this_column[$count]')};
$sth = $dbh->prepare($query);
$sth->execute();
++$count;
};
```

We declared a count and declared a foreach loop that will iterate until the length of @this_column is reached. We then declared the query and put it in $query. The query was then prepared for execution using prepare(). We executed the query using execute() and incremented the $count for the next iteration of the loop.

31

Note that we used the three-step method of performing your database query. There are two other methods that may be used to have your query declared, prepared, and executed, as shown in Listing 2-7.

***Listing 2-7.*** Using the two-step method to INSERT from an array

```
$count = "0";
foreach (@this_column) {
$sth = $dbh->prepare(INSERT INTO this_table (col1) VALUES ('$this_
column[$count]'));
$sth->execute();
++$count;
};
```

The preceding example task shows the two-step method of achieving a successful insertion query. You can see that we eliminated the $query scalar variable and instead passed the query as the argument to the prepare() function. The execute() function was then called. This handy method is used extensively because it results in a clean query that uses less resources than does the three-step method.

In our previous examples, we used the prepare() function to handle the query. Listing 2-8 provides a one-step method that can be used that omits both the prepare() and execute() functions entirely.

***Listing 2-8.*** Using the one-step method to INSERT from an array

```
$count = "0";
foreach (@this_column) {
$sth = $dbh->do(INSERT INTO this_table (col1) VALUES ('$this_
column[$count]'));
++$count;
};
```

Using the do() method of performing your query is a handy one liner that is both useful and powerful. With it, you may perform any valid MySQL query.

So we've explored an insertion from an array using the three-step, two-step, and one-step methods of performing your database query. These easy statements are the core of any web developer's plethora of tricks and constructions.

The simple insertion statements we've explored here can just as easily be very complicated JOIN statements that utilize the full power and flexibility of this duo of programming languages. The limit is your understanding of the languages and the needs of your situation. While big, powerful JOINs can be fun to work with, keep things simple and use the simplest method for achieving your desired end result. You'll thank me when you have to work with a script that you created a year before and are expected to understand it.

## Inserting Many Database Items from Many Arrays

The time will come when you require a large, multi-array insertion into your database. What we'll explore in this section are the ways that you may insert the data that exists in many arrays into your database. The introduction of more arrays into the equation isn't a bad thing; we're just starting to learn the tremendous flexibility of this combination of programming tools.

We'll begin by defining several fictitious arrays, each of the same length. The data may be textual/ASCII or binary. Note, though, that you would have to create the column using the right column type. Column types are beyond the scope of this section, so we'll assume all the data we're working with is textual only and is being put into VARCHAR or BLOB column types.

The easiest way to insert the data from many arrays into your database is to loop through the arrays with a foreach loop. You would declare a $count that is initially set to zero. This is because all arrays within Perl are zero based. They're indexed according to a number system that starts with zero. With Perl, zero is a whole number (an integer).

For each iteration of the loop, more than one array is being referred to. This results in a potentially massive amount of data being inserted into the database. Be sure to limit yourself to 300 or 400 iterations, although more can be used if the amount of data is fairly small for each insertion and your server has plenty of resources. You may have as many row and column insertions as you need – this construction is infinitely scalable. Use a LIMIT declaration to limit the amount of database rows to be created if that is required.

You may use either a foreach loop or a while loop to achieve the same result. Use a while loop when you have a specific number of rows to be inserted. That is, if you know beforehand how many rows are to be inserted, then use while. If you have a varying amount of database rows to be inserted, use the foreach loop to iterate through your gathered arrays.

# Using a foreach Loop to Insert Many Items from Many Arrays

You can see in the example task given in Listing 2-9 that for each element of @col1, we looped through the index items of three arrays (@col1, @col2, and @col3) due to the iteration of $count. The example assumes you have three arrays of equal length for each table column. The rows are inserted one at a time and perfectly reflect the array data.

*Listing 2-9.* Using a foreach loop with an insertion

```
$count = "0";
foreach (@col1) {
$query = qq{INSERT INTO this_table (
     col1,
     col2,
     col3
) VALUES (
      '$col1[$count]',
      '$col2[$count]',
      '$col3[$count]'
)}";
$sth = $dbh->prepare($query);
$sth->execute();
     ++$count;
};
```

We declare the $count and set it to zero. The foreach loop was then declared, and we used @col1 as the argument. We can use @col1 as the argument because every array is of the same length – no data will be left out of the insertion. We declared the query and stored it in $query. We then prepared the query using prepare(). We executed the query using execute() and incremented the $count for the next iteration of the loop, starting the process over and inserting more data.

Note that I've used a more vertical approach to ordering my query, putting each element of the query on its own line. With Perl, you can break up the more complicated code into more readable forms. This is mine. You'll find yours. Note also that in order

for this approach to be possible, you wouldn't use double quotes to define your query –
double quotes only work when the entire query is on one line. Nest your query within
the Perl qq{} statements to allow your query to span more than one line.

You can see how powerful and intuitive are the workings of the Perl DBI module.
With it, you are able to store and retrieve any data from the database. While we used very
simple examples as learning tools, there is essentially no limit on how complicated and
capable your future DBI machinations can be. The limit is your skill and imagination –
Perl and MySQL are up to the task.

# Summary

In this chapter, we covered the various ways that Perl and the DBI module work together
to do some very powerful operations. We explored database structures and the means to
select or insert the data in question.

# CHAPTER 3

# Essential MySQL Skills

Before we start delving into the scripts that make up the project for this book, we should first cover a few bases. In this chapter, we'll review the skills necessary in order to make sense of what is to come. You may already be familiar with these concepts, but it is always a good idea to review a skill before having to apply it to a live, functioning script.

In this chapter, we'll work through the functions that will be used in the project. We'll cover only those functions that will be used in the project – we won't cover all of the abilities that the DBI module offers, for example.

## MySQL Column and Index Types

Within MySQL are many different types of data that you can tailor your database tables to accept. Everything from common text characters to binary information may be provided for. Any valid data type can be used. A valid type is number or string, for example.

Column types are declared upon creation of a table. There are many different types, and we'll cover them all in the sections to come. While we won't be using every column type in the projects, it is of paramount importance that you know and understand the full breadth of what is available. This knowledge will come in handy if you plan on expanding one of the projects, a full featured bulletin board.

## Integer Column Types

We'll start with the integer column types. The integer column types are a numeric type of column and are used to store numbers only – if you try to insert text, MySQL will throw an error.

© Thomas Valentine 2023
T. Valentine, *Database-Driven Web Development*, https://doi.org/10.1007/978-1-4842-9792-6_3

There is a very wide range of integer types – the full range of signed numbers available is huge. By signed, I mean the negative numbers are represented. Note that the positive number is one less than the negatively signed number. This is because the number zero is still considered an integer. Zero is a value – it is not to be confused with the null value, which is considered to be an absence of value.

# Floating-Point Column Types

A floating-point column type is simply a column type that includes a decimal point. The decimal point may "float" from one position to another, hence the floating point name.

Floating-point numbers are usually used when the range of numbers from an integer column type isn't high or low enough for the task at hand. It should be noted that floating-point numbers are approximate values – MySQL will round the floating-point number to the number of decimal places you define when the table is created.

# Character String Column Types

Character strings are either CHAR or VARCHAR. CHAR stands for "Characters," and VARCHAR stands for "Varying Characters." A fixed length for the column is set during table creation. If the data is not as long as the length of the declared CHAR or VARCHAR, the space remaining is padded with spaces. It should be noted that if the value you've inserted has trailing spaces by design, the spaces will be removed. You'll have to provide for this within the Perl script in order to add the trailing spaces.

If you need a binary columned case-sensitive CHAR or VARCHAR column, set this with the BINARY flag. If the BINARY flag is present, the column is case sensitive when used for sorting or comparison. Otherwise, strings are case insensitive.

# BLOB Column Types

BLOB column types are of varying width. BLOB stands for Binary Large Object. They are able to store very large data sets and don't trim trailing spaces. A BLOB column is case sensitive. Values that exceed the maximum length are simply truncated. BLOBs cannot have default values.

# Enumeration or Set Column Types

Enumerations and sets are string columns that have a small set of possible values. If no value is declared upon table creation, an empty string will be inserted. The ENUM column type has a maximum value of 64 KB (65535 bytes), and the SET column type has a maximum value of 64 bytes.

To insert a value in an ENUM column, use a string literal. That is, encase the string within quotes. To insert multiple values in a SET column, separate the values within the opening and closing quotes with commas.

# Time Column Types

MySQL provides a wide array of date and time stamps. The time is taken from the operating system of the server the MySQL database resides upon.

MySQL is able to use time and date stamps in an ORDER BY clause, so you're able to sort your data by both date and time. This great feature comes in handy if you're looking to order the contents of a table by date or time or both.

All time and date values are integers. If, for some reason, you should have a floating-point number as part of a date, MySQL will round to the nearest value of the following: month values are limited to 1 to 12. Day values are limited to 1 to 31. Hour values are from 0 to 23, while minutes and seconds range in value from 0 to 59.

# Perl and MySQL Functions Review

Reviewing a skill, no matter its depth, is always a good thing as you will always come away with a new vantage point. In this section, we'll be reviewing the specific skills that will be used in the project which we'll begin working on in the coming chapters.

There is always more than one way to do something with Perl, syntactically speaking. Because of this, I'll try to present each topic in this section in more than one way.

# Creating Tables

Creating a table is a straightforward affair, but there are a few things that you need to know first. We'll use the three-step method to create our tables. We visited this three-step method in Chapter 2.

When creating a table, you will first need to know the column types that you'll be using. You will also need to know the names of the columns. Column names are case sensitive, remember, so name your columns accordingly.

In the project to come, the primary key is the first column, named "id." It is an autoincrement column, as you can see in the example of a table creation given in Listing 3-1.

*Listing 3-1.* Creating a table using both Perl and MySQL

```
$query = qq{CREATE TABLE $thisthread (
     id INT AUTO_INCREMENT PRIMARY KEY,
     title VARCHAR (250) NOT NULL,
     threadid VARCHAR (20) NOT NULL,
     posts VARCHAR (20) NOT NULL,
     date VARCHAR (20) NOT NULL
     )};
$sth = $dbh->prepare($query);
$sth->execute();
```

As you can see, creating a table is a simple but very powerful function. The id column is an integer and is the primary key of the table. The other VARCHAR columns range in size from 20 to 250 characters. The 20-character limited columns are numbers and the date, all of which will not exceed 20 characters in length. The title column is set to 250 characters, as it is the title of a thread. The maximum character count (defined in a different script within the project) is 250 characters because it is a descriptive column of the table – the thread name may be up to 250 characters. You'll see this table creation in putnewthread.cgi within the project we'll soon be working on, so I won't show any more of the code for now. Please focus on the table structure within the Perl code.

# Loops

The most common functions we'll be using in the project are simple loops. We'll be constructing lists that are accrued via the use of a loop that selects data from the database and formats it into an HTML segment. This segment of HTML and the data from the database are then added to the final results and are displayed in the user's browser.

There are two forms of loops used in the project: the foreach() loop and the while() loop. Each is used in slightly different ways and locations, as you'll see in the coming discussions.

## The while( ) Loop

The while() loop is used to select one piece of data at a time. If there is only one result, it is placed in a scalar variable. If there are multiple results, the data is pushed onto an array, as given in Listing 3-2.

***Listing 3-2.*** Performing a while loop

```
$query = "SELECT id FROM $thistopic WHERE id >= 0 ";
$sth = $dbh->prepare($query);
$sth->execute;
while ($thisvalue = $sth->fetchrow()) {
    push @theseids, $thisvalue;
};
```

The while() loop iterates until there are no more results being pushed onto the array by MySQL. Note that the primary key, id, is being selected. You'll see a lot of that in the scripts to follow.

## The foreach( ) Loop

We use the foreach() loop mostly to construct the final HTML markup that will be displayed to the user, although that is not the only place it is used. It can also be used to loop through table rows via a previous database call. Using the id column as a means to limit your database queries is a good place to use a foreach() loop, as shown in Listing 3-3.

***Listing 3-3.*** A fully functional foreach loop

```
$count = "0";
foreach (@theseids) {
    $query = qq{SELECT title, threadid, posts, date
        FROM $thistopic
```

```
            WHERE id = $theseids[$count] LIMIT 30};
    $sth = $dbh->prepare($query);
    $sth->execute();
    while (@thisvalue = $sth->fetchrow_array()) {
            push @titles, $thisvalue[0];
            push @threadids, $thisvalue[1];
            push @posts, $thisvalue[2];
            push @date, $thisvalue[3];
    }
++$count;
};
```

This code snippet was taken from threads.cgi. It shows a foreach() loop that will iterate through the loop as long as there is a value (a previously gathered array based on the id primary key) within @theseids. You can also see that a while() loop is being used to gather data from the database based on the $theseids[$count] array. We'll delve further into the workings of a construction such as this in a later chapter. For now, this basic construction has been an example of what is to come in terms of loops.

# Pushing an Array

By "pushing" an array, it means that a value is being added to the end of an array. An array can be likened to a list, with each list item being given an index number, starting at zero. Every time you push an array, you're adding to the end of the list. The syntax for pushing an array is as follows:

```
push @thisarray, $thisvariable;
```

The scalar variable $thisvariable is being added to the end of the list, that is, @thisarray. Simple. We'll be using this snippet of code in almost every script within the project, so it is important that you understand the process now before we start examining code in great detail.

# Gathering Content

Every script we'll be using is a collection of individual sets of data that have been formatted into HTML markup. In collecting the data, you do so in a fashion that is conducive to being easily formatted. What is usually done once the data is collected is the data is placed in the logically ordered HTML markup, which can be text within a table or anchor tag links, although you are not limited to just those two options. Examine the snippet of code given in Listing 3-4.

***Listing 3-4.*** Gathering content to be displayed

```
$count = "0";
foreach (@these_ids) {
        $oneContentElement = qq{<TR ><TD ALIGN="CENTER" VALIGN="TOP">
        <A HREF= "/cgi-bin/this_script.cgi?id=$id[$count]& id2=$id2[$count]"
        >$thislink[$count] </A></TD></TR>};
        push @endarray, oneContentElement;
        ++$count;
};
```

First, a $count is declared and is set to zero. We then initiated a foreach() loop using @these_ids as the argument. The newly declared scalar variable, $oneContentElement, is stuffed with some HTML markup. Notice that there are three separate and distinct arrays being used (@id, @id2, and @thislink). Each array's index items are used as the unique data for every iteration of @these_ids. Since the $count is being incremented every time the loop iterates, the data within each of the three arrays (three links) changes and is pushed onto @endarray.

It is the entire HTML markup that is pushed onto @endarray that is to be displayed in the user's browser. This example contains only the code for three links. In the project to come, we'll be adding images, links, and other useful page elements to the mix.

# Ordering Your Arrays: Perl reverse( ) vs. MySQL ASC or DESC

In working with an array, it is sometimes favorable to reverse it and apply formatting to the data that has been reversed. There are three options available: one via Perl and two via MySQL.

The Perl reverse() function is one such option. You would apply the reversal to every array that you are working with. This takes MySQL out of the loop and is sometimes favorable in situations where you've already retrieved data from the database. Use the reverse() method as follows:

```
@this_new_array = reverse(@this_array);
```

You can see how easy it is to use the reverse() function. It is equally easy to use the ASC (ascending) and DESC (descending) clauses via MySQL. Examine the following examples:

```
$query = qq{SELECT fieldone, fieldtwo FROM this_table
    ORDER BY id ASC};
```

Or

```
$query = qq{SELECT fieldone, fieldtwo FROM this_table
    ORDER BY id DESC};
```

Each MySQL statement uses the id primary key to organize the data returned – what direction the data is actually retrieved from is a function of the ASC or DESC clauses.

DESC orders the information in a descending manner. That is, the data that is at the top of the table is also the oldest. A descending order returns the data organized from the oldest data on the top of the list to the newest data on the bottom of the list. The ASC clause places the oldest data at the bottom of the list, leaving the newest data at the top of the list.

There are pros and cons for all three methods of ordering your data. While the Perl reverse() function is useful, it is the slowest of the three methods. The ASC and DESC methods are faster, since MySQL is written in a faster programming language optimized for this kind of operation and is already memory resident. What method to use is entirely up to you – tailor to your situation.

# Links and Parameters

We'll be using loaded links extensively in the upcoming project sections. A loaded link is one that contains parameters that scripts use to pass on data that is used to retrieve data for the next page. An example of a loaded link is as follows:

```
<A HREF="/cgi-bin/this_script.cgi?id=1234&id2=5678">This Link</A>
```

This method of loading links is the GET method, as you'll remember from a previous chapter. The id parameter holds the value 1234, and the id2 parameter holds the value 5678. These parameters and their associated values are what are used to generate the page that is generated by the "this_script.cgi" script.

# Summary

This chapter covered data types and how to both insert and retrieve large amounts of data. The concept of ordering your arrays via the Perl reverse() method and the MySQL ASC and DESC attributes was explored. We then performed several possibly large inserts into a database.

# CHAPTER 4

# Nuts and Bolts

With all that you have learned so far, there are still a few things that you need to know to get the job done. This chapter introduces the skills needed for you to expand your working knowledge of database-driven web development.

We'll begin with simple date and time formatting and move on to more involved topics, such as gathering your data and presenting it to your users via the browser. Most of these concepts were introduced as examples of code in previous chapters. They were kept as simple as possible to enable you to learn. From now on, I'll be using actual functioning code from the example projects we'll be discussing in the coming chapters. There's a lot to cover, so let's get to work.

## Date and Time Formatting

There are a number of different Perl modules that can be used to present the date and time to your users. These modules are usually very hefty and slow, and to be honest, they aren't required in most cases. This is because you can take the date and time directly from the operating system using the backtick operator (`). The backtick operator is used to make system calls to whatever operating system you're using.

These modules all use the backtick operator to retrieve the date and time eventually, so you can speed things up by doing it yourself. We'll stick to Linux date and time, as this is the most prevalent operating system used on Internet servers.

You might be asking why there are so many different Perl modules just to format the date and time. The answer is there are simply many ways to present the date and time. This is what the date and time modules do – format what they get from a system call for the date and time into something a little more presentable. The reason they're so large is because they have many different ways to present the date and time all in one module. All of this complication translates into a slow functioning Perl module.

© Thomas Valentine 2023
T. Valentine, *Database-Driven Web Development*, https://doi.org/10.1007/978-1-4842-9792-6_4

The system call syntax to retrieve the date and time on Linux is very simple. Examine the following code snippet:

```
$date = `date`;
```

On Linux, the "date" command brings up both the date and time down to the last second. In this case, these date and time are stored in the $date variable, which now contains the following:

```
Fri Nov 20 11:18:44 PST 2023
```

You can see that a full representation of both the date and time is given. This might not be what you'd like to see as your date or time – this is true in most cases. What we need to do now is format the date and time into something more aesthetically pleasing. You can do this very simply with the concatenation operator (.) and the split() function, as shown in Listing 4-1.

***Listing 4-1.*** Formatting $date

```
@date_raw   = split(/ /, $date);
$date_complete = $date_raw[0] . ", " . $date_raw[1] . " " .  $date_raw[2] .
", " . " " . $date_raw[5];
```

What I just did is split the contents of $date on the spaces with the split function and pushed the results into the @date_raw array. I then created $date_complete and concatenated index numbers 0, 1, 2, and 5 to come to the formatted date:

```
Fri, Nov 20, 2023
```

You can see that I didn't use the time and time zone, which reside in index items 3 and 4 ($date_raw[3] and $date_raw[4]). You can also see from within the concatenations that I've added commas between index items 0 and 1 and 2 and 5.

# Website Parameters

You'll eventually need to include parameters in your scripts. Catching and using your parameters is a common occurrence, so you'll have to fully understand their use.

Know a website parameter as the jumble of letters, numbers, and special characters that come after the question mark (?) following the file name:

```
http://www.domain.com/cgi-bin/script.cgi?id=123456&id2=abcdefg
```

As you can see, the fully qualified domain name given holds two parameters and a file name. The parameters given are the id and id2 parameters. They each hold values and are separated by an ampersand (&). You may have as many parameters as needed, with the usual maximum being about half a dozen parameters.

This particular parameter method is known as the GET method. There is another method of submitting parameters called the POST method. These concepts were visited briefly in a past chapter.

In order to use the POST method, you must submit the parameters from within an HTML form element, as shown in Listing 4-2.

**Listing 4-2.** Using a FORM with the method set to POST

```
<FORM NAME="form1" METHOD="POST" ACTION=" http://www.domain.com/cgi-bin/
script.cgi">
      <INPUT TYPE="hidden" NAME="id" VALUE="123456">
      <INPUT TYPE="hidden" NAME="id2" VALUE="abcdefg">
      <INPUT TYPE="submit" VALUE="Submit Values">
</FORM>
```

You can see from the preceding example that I've inserted the parameters within opening and closing HTML form elements in type "hidden" INPUTs. The parameters will be uploaded to the server when the Submit button is clicked.

Since the method of POST is used, the parameters will be passed to the server within the message body instead of within the values in the address bar.

# Catching the Parameters

The easiest way to catch a parameter is with the param() method, which is within the capabilities of the CGI module. In order to invoke the param() method, you must first create a new instance of the CGI module, as shown in Listing 4-3.

**Listing 4-3.** Catching parameters using the param() method

```
USE CGI;
$cgi = new CGI;
$id = $cgi->param('id');
$id2 = $cgi->param('id2');
```

You can see that I first included a "USE CGI;" statement. I then created a new instance of the CGI module through the use of the "$cgi = new CGI;" statement. The id and id2 parameters were then caught with the "$id = $cgi->param('id');" and "$id2 = $cgi->param('id2');" methods, the values of which are now stored in $id and $id2. It should be noted that the parameter names are case sensitive.

You may have as many parameters as necessary, with the limit being between five and ten in one script. It should be noted that the POST method can pass more parameters than can the GET method.

## Processing the Parameters

There are many ways of processing a parameter. What I've found is that regular expressions are used often and can be applied to the data contained in the parameter's variable in order to combat malicious attacks.

A regular expression that only allows numbers to be within a parameter's variable:

```
$id =~ s/[A-Za-z\s]+//g;
```

As you can see in the regular expression, all letters will be stripped from the variable, $id. This allows only numbers to be contained within the parameter's variable. Malicious users won't have a chance to hack your script because it is impossible to gain entrance to a script without using textual commands in some way.

You may also put the parameter's values directly into a database if security isn't an issue. Since a parameter has a logical use, you may prepare your data to be used in the next script or format it to be able to access a particular database table, with the parameter's value being the unique identifier. Consider the following example:

```
$profileid = $id . "profile";
```

I used the concatenation operator again to join the $id and the word "profile" in quotes. Note that the word "profile" is contained within opening and closing double quotes. This tells Perl that the contents are textual in nature. The $profileid variable now holds the following value:

```
123456profile
```

Since the new variable $profileid is now a unique value, you may use it to access a unique database table or row within a table, in this case, the site profile of that particular user.

# Loading Your Links

There will come a time when using an HTML form to pass your parameters just will not work. It is not always possible to use a form and the POST method. In this case, you have to work out a way to pass your data via the GET method of loading your links. In this case, you can load your links with data.

As touched on in an earlier section of this chapter, data can be carried from page to page via a loaded link:

```
/cgi-bin/script.cgi?id1=123456id2=abcdef
```

The loading of your links should be very familiar to you now. It is important that you understand how to load your links since it is a technique that is used with almost every Perl script.

In the following sections, we'll take your knowledge of loading links further so you are able to create loaded links dynamically, according to database entries from multiple Perl arrays.

# Gathering the Information

Gathering all of the information from your database into multiple arrays is a straightforward affair that uses the fetchrow_array() method. What we'll be doing is gathering all of the information from one table. Examine the construction given in Listing 4-4.

*Listing 4-4.* Gathering data for later formatting

```
$query = qq{SELECT id1, id2, id3, id4 FROM thistable
    WHERE id >= 0};
$sth = $dbh->prepare($query);
$sth->execute();
while (@thisvalue = $sth->fetchrow_array()) {
```

```
    push @id1, $thisvalue[0];
    push @id2, $thisvalue[1];
    push @id3, $thisvalue[2];
    push @id4, $thisvalue[3];
};
```

So we've gathered all of the information from one table and placed the contents of each column into its own array via the use of the Perl push function. We now have a complete representation of the database table within the @id1, @id2, @id3, and @id4 arrays. Read on to find out what to do with them.

## Constructing the End Array

What we'll be doing with the arrays generated in the previous section is construct loaded links dynamically using the contents of the four arrays. We'll be placing the database information within one large array using the functions given in Listing 4-5.

*Listing 4-5.* Gathering the end results

```
$count = 0;
foreach (@id1) {
$oneContentElement = qq{<tr>
<td align="right" valign="top">
    <a href="thesmessages.cgi?id1=$id1($count]&id2=$id2[$count]&id3=id3
    [$count]&id4=$id4[$count]">Message[$count]</a>
</td>
</tr>};
push @contentArray, $oneContentElement;
++$count;
};
```

We started by declaring $count. We set its value to 0. The reason why we did this will be addressed in the paragraphs to come.

We then declared a foreach() loop using @id1 as the argument. In this case, it is used as a count to dictate how many times the foreach() loop will be iterated.

As you can see from the HTML markup within the $oneContentElement variable, there are four parameters given to each anchor element. The $count refers to the index item position within each array.

For example, the first index item within @id1 is zero, since we haven't iterated the $count from its original value of zero yet.

This set of links is then pushed onto @contentArray, and then we iterated $count. $count now has the value of 1.

Since we have now reached the end of the construction, it is then looped through again, this time with different values being pushed onto @contentArray due to $count being iterated.

The entire construction is looped through with $count being iterated for each loop. The construction will loop until the @id1 array is out of index items to trigger another iteration and push onto @contentArray.

# The External Content Template

Now that you have the necessary knowledge to generate and format page content, you must now learn how to generate a full HTML page that the contents of @contentArray will be printed within.

To do this, you must create a new Perl script with HTML markup within it. Place this markup within a variable enclosed with a double quote operator (qq{}). We use a double quote operator because it allows more than a single line of code to be encapsulated within it, as is the case with the textual double quote (").

The only Perl code that is put in this script is one variable and the shebang, which is used to tell the script where to find Perl. The following is an example of a common shebang:

```
#!/usr/bin/perl
```

The name of the variable I always use in this situation is $htmlContent. An example of a very simple external content template is shown in Listing 4-6.

*Listing 4-6.* An external content template

```
#!/usr/bin/perl
$htmlContent = qq{<!DOCTYPE HTML>
<head>
```

```
<title> - - - Web Site Title - - - </title>
<body >
<table border="0" cellpadding="0" cellspacing="0" align="center"
width="100%">
@contentArray
</table>
</body>
</html>};
1;
```

The preceding shown markup is simplified in order to learn without too much complication. However, it is still a valid and complete page of HTML markup.

We first started with the shebang, followed by the $htmlContent variable, which is stated between opening and closing qq{} operators.

We then moved on to some simple markup and ended the script with a number 1. The number 1 is required in order to return a value of true to Perl. Leaving this number out will cause a fatal error to be thrown, ending execution of the script.

You might have noticed that I included the @contentArray array between the opening and closing table elements. The table element markup meshes with the four simple links we used in an earlier section of this chapter.

Stating @contentArray in this way will allow you to have more complicated pages that utilize the content generated with the loading of your links discussed in detail in a previous section of this chapter.

In order for the HTML content template to be used with the rest of your script, simply utilize a Perl require statement:

```
require "content.pl";
```

The key to this system is declaring the require statement at the very end of your Perl script. This way, all of your data has been collected and formatted and is ready to be printed to the user's browser.

## Printing the End Array

Printing your content to the user's browser is simple and straightforward. It is the last command given within a script and will appear on the last lines of the script:

```
print qq{Content-type: text/html\n\n};
print qq{$htmlcontent};
```

You can see that we first told the browser what type of data that is to be received and displayed with the Content-type command. We used "text/html\n\n" as the content type that is to be received by the browser.

Now everything comes together. The data that is collected from the database is formatted and pushed on to @contentArray. @contentArray is then put within an appropriate place in the external content template, content.pl. The variable with all of the markup within it is then printed to the browser. Simple.

# Using the CGI::Carp Module

Every script has an error in it after you've completed writing it. A script of any complexity will have at least one error within it.

While Perl can't correct your mistakes, it does allow you a means as to what the problem is. To that end, the CGI::Carp module is an invaluable tool that is used to help you find your errors. As with all Perl modules, it is declared at the top of the script. The following is its syntax:

```
use CGI::Carp qw(fatalsToBrowser);
```

As you can see, declaring it is a simple matter. Instead of having to use the command prompt to debug your scripts, the CGI::Carp module will print your errors to the browser. The reports are very intuitive and easy to figure out.

The reports announce the error, the script, and the line number of the script where the fatal error occurred.

You would normally use this module during development of the site. After you have all site errors figured out, it is recommended that you comment out CGI::Carp so your users won't be able to figure out your scripting or database model. Leaving CGI::Carp active with a live script opens you to attacks from malicious users.

# Username and Password Maintenance

Username and password maintenance is an important part of developing your website. Unless you use a secure shell connection (which is beyond the scope of this book), you would normally use FTP to place your files where they should be.

Changing your password once a month will allow you peace of mind, knowing that other developers won't be able to access your site's critical files. Creating a new account with a different username will also add to the security of your site.

When it comes to database usernames and passwords, changing the username and password is usually a big chore, as all of the database calls will fail unless you change the username and password of the connection statement. You would have to change the username and password of every Perl script that uses a database.

If you only have a small number of scripts running on your site, changing the username and password would be a viable security effort.

Instead of changing the username and password in your database connection script, use a well-crafted password. A good password in this case is 10 to 12 characters long.

Use letters of both cases, numbers, and punctuation in your password to reduce the chances of someone gaining access via your database connection statement. It should be noted that both the username and password are case sensitive on MySQL.

# Per-User Usage Statistics

On some sites, tracking users is a required operation. This is usually the case if the site is a charge-for-service site where the user pays according to what services they utilize.

Tracking a user is most easily done via their IP address. Tracking an IP (Internet Protocol) address is made easy with the CGI module. Consider the following:

```
$userip = $cgi->remote_host();
```

This statement will return the user's IP address, allowing you to record it or work upon it at will. Some sites narrow a user's address using the IP address, allowing them to record your general location or use it in a sales pitch.

Tracking the pages each user uses is a common feature of many sites. By tracking users' movements, it is possible to know which sections of your site are being used and which ones aren't being used. This will allow you to make informed changes to those site features that aren't being utilized.

Tracking your users requires a database call or two. There are two methods that are commonly used to record if a script and thus a page of your site are being accessed. The first is a straightforward two-step method, as given in Listing 4-7.

***Listing 4-7.*** A hit counter using MySQL

```
$query = qq{SELECT hits FROM tracker};
$sth = $dbh->prepare($query);
$sth->execute();
$thisHit = $sth->fetchrow()
};
++$thisHit;
$query = qq{UPDATE tracker SET hits = '$thisHit'};
$sth = $dbh->prepare($query);
$sth->execute();
};
```

You can see that two database calls were carried out. First, the hit count is fetched using the upper statement. We then incremented that retrieved value and updated the new value into the database. This is a good, straightforward way of recording a single page hit.

The single call method is perhaps the more elegant of the two methods. With it, you only use one database call and let MySQL do the work for you:

```
$query = qq{UPDATE tracker SET hits + 1};
$sth = $dbh->prepare($query);
$sth->execute();
};
```

As you can see, a single Perl call results in a cleaner script, also allowing the faster executing MySQL to do the increment for you.

# Deleting Tables

Deleting tables can be a risky affair, especially because MySQL doesn't have a reliable restore feature. Once a table is deleted, it is gone for good, so some care has to be taken. You would normally drop a table via scripted action. Make sure that the proper validity checks are taken before the table is dropped.

For example, if a user is deleting their account, the table(s) should be dropped after checking that the rest of the deletion script has been evaluated and a table deletion is found to be the case. You may then drop a table successfully.

The proper term for deleting a table is "dropping" the table, and this is reflected in the syntax of the database call, as the following shows:

```
$query = qq{DROP TABLE username_master};
$sth = $dbh->prepare($query);
$sth->execute();
```

As you can see, a table deletion is simple and has a minimum of clutter. Also, make sure you're dropping the right table or troubles will ensue.

# Deleting Rows

Deleting a row in a table is a common practice and is usually completed via scripted action. Deleting an entire row in a database can be done by matching a value within the row, telling MySQL which row to delete that way.

As I've said before, always have an autoincrement id column present in every table. Since this id table starts at zero and works upward from there (hence the term autoincrement), it is a very safe way to identify one single row for deletion, even in a table with thousands of entries.

To narrow down which row to delete among thousands, you would use a WHERE clause. Simply match which row to delete via the id column and it'll be a safe bet that you've deleted the intended row within the table.

Examine the example of a row deletion in Listing 4-8 where the row to delete is found via the row's id column.

*Listing 4-8.* Deleting a row

```
$query = qq{DELETE thisrow FROM master WHERE id = 1234};
$sth = $dbh->prepare($query);
$sth->execute();
```

You can see how and where to use a WHERE clause in your database call. I used the values 1234 as the row identifier in the example. It is an entirely possible, and oft-used, method of deletion to use a variable instead of a static row name such as shown in the example.

Note also that we used the id column name to come to the decision to delete that row. I've found this method to be invaluable when working with a database of any flavor.

# Uploading Files

Uploading files is perhaps the most complicated operation you'll run across in your dealings with Perl and MySQL. The actual Perl script you would use to upload a file is beyond the current chapters of this book, but you have to be aware of a few things before you can start thinking about an upload script for future use.

The first thing to consider when you're working with file uploading is that the HTML form element must reflect the fact that a file is to be uploaded. Examine the following HTML form statement:

```
<form method="post" action="upload_script.cgi" enctype="multipart/
form-data">
    <input type="file" name="photo">
    <input type="submit" value="Upload Image">
</form>
```

As you can see, there are a couple of things to include in a form that wouldn't usually be there. The first is the ENCTYPE, which in the example is set to "multipart/form-data". This tells the browser, then the server, that an upload of several parts is being uploaded. The first part is the ENCTYPE, which will hold the name of the file as well as a different data container that will hold the digital coding of the file itself.

The next part of the form that has changed is the type, which is set to "file". This tells the browser to display a form element that has a Select button and a small space to show the file name.

Click the "Select" button, and a dialog box appears with your computer's file system shown within it. Navigate to the desired file, click it once to select it, and click the OK button.

The file name, now selected, will be displayed next to the button. Click the Submit button and your file will be uploaded to the script given in the form.

Depending on your browser, you should see a progress indicator somewhere that shows, as a percentage of the total size of the file, how much of the file has been uploaded and therefore how much more that has to still be uploaded.

# Managing Images and Files

Managing files via scripted action can be confusing for the newbie developer. While there are many Perl modules that can be used to manage your file collection, you don't have to use them. Once again, use the backtick (') operator. The backtick operator allows you to make system calls directly to the server's operating system. Most Internet servers run the Linux operating system, so all of the database calls we'll make in the coming chapters will reflect this.

In web development, for every file, there are two locations. The first is the URL, which is the file's location that your users will see via the browser. The second is the file's location within the server's operating system.

We'll be primarily working with the latter file location – the place the file resides on the server. All Linux servers use basically the same commands when it comes to dealing with files, so do use the backtick operator liberally.

# Summary

This was a fun chapter. We explored date and time formatting, loading your links, and the external content template. A few SQL commands were studied, and we discussed concerns regarding gathering your database-generated content and applying HTML markup. We also opened discussions on file and image uploads, topics that will be expanded in the chapters to come.

# CHAPTER 5

# Understanding the Document Object Model (DOM)

Now that we've covered the basics, we'll delve into the intricacies of the Document Object Model, or DOM for short. As its name implies, DOM is the process of accessing and perhaps changing the properties of the individual objects that comprise your HTML document.

Every object in your page has a certain set of properties associated with it. Those properties are the equivalent of the attributes of a page element. Each of these attributes or rules may be changed or set by a simple DOM statement or by a more in-depth JavaScript function. We'll concentrate for the time being on the more simple DOM statements, accumulating your knowledge until a JavaScript function will make sense to you, the reader.

You'll see as you progress through the following chapters that the specific implementation of the DOM language is different from browser to browser and from operating system platform to platform. In this section of this book, you'll see that some of the DOM statements for the major browsers differ slightly in their implementation. The valid DOM statements for each browser are included with the reference for each object, property, method, and event handler.

In an effort to alleviate the confusion caused by the individual implementations of DOM by the major browsers, the W3C is working on a universal standard which will hopefully be embraced by the major browser vendors. Until then, we'll just have to slug it out with the varying uses and implementations of DOM and its associated languages.

© Thomas Valentine 2023
T. Valentine, *Database-Driven Web Development*, https://doi.org/10.1007/978-1-4842-9792-6_5

Within the DOM specifications, there are five separate components that are used to construct a valid and complete DOM statement. They are as follows:

1. Objects

2. Methods

3. Arrays

4. Properties

5. Values

While you most likely won't use all of the preceding components in one statement, you must know and understand the capabilities of each. The easiest way to learn is to just dive right in. With that in mind, consider the following valid DOM statement. Try to spot the HTML tag and attribute which this statement reflects. Drawing on the knowledge gleaned from previous chapters, you'll find that it is very easy to do.

```
document.body.alink = "red"
```

This DOM statement changes or sets the color of the "active link" to be used within the entire page. Did you spot the BODY tag and its attribute, "alink"? This is what DOM is all about – reflecting the existing commands that are part of your finished web page. Using these reflections, you may change or set the values for almost every page element and attribute, including CSS rules.

The "document" part of the preceding statement is an object that represents the entire page contents – the entire "document". The browser, in implementing DOM, sees the complete web page as an object that is the container for other objects, methods, or arrays. The "body" part of the preceding statement is an object within the "document" object. The "alink" is a property of the "body" object, and the "red" after the equals sign is a value of the property, "alink". This hierarchical approach is common to all DOM statements.

Every HTML tag and every CSS rule have an object associated with it. The object itself is what is accessed when stating a value of a property – the property is one of the values of the object. There are about 120 objects within the DOM specifications, with about 400 properties that are used to describe the action that is to be assigned to the object. There are about 100 methods and 16 arrays. The total number of event handlers is about 40. The amount of values that are available is just too high to attempt to count, easily numbering in the thousands.

In your use of the DOM specifications, it is extremely important to be able to distinguish an object from a method, and a property from an object. Spotting the DOM method is simple – the statement is completed with opening and closing brackets. Often there is a value nested within the brackets. The array is completed with opening and closing square brackets, while the value is enclosed within quotes, acting as the terminator of the statement. Spot the object within a statement by the fact that the object name is often the exact HTML element name whose functionality it reflects.

The easiest way to distinguish an object from a property is to draw on your knowledge from the preceding chapters. Every page element has an object, attribute, and a property. That is, the properties of an object are often the exact terms used as the attribute name in HTML.

The CSS rules and values reflected within the Document Object Model are accessed through the "style" object – any statements following the "style" object must be the DOM equivalent of a CSS rule. The values of the rule are placed after the equals sign, enclosed within quotes.

# The DOM Statement

With DOM, you may change colors, set borders, create flying objects, define draggable screen objects, and just about anything else you can dream up. All HTML tags, attributes, and event handlers as well as all CSS rules and values may be accessed through the Document Object Model. Using DOM statements, you may actually construct your entire document without using HTML or CSS commands, though it isn't practical because of DOM's high cost in terms of bandwidth. DOM simply isn't meant to be used to build whole pages with – some HTML and CSS are a requirement. The following example shows perhaps the simplest valid DOM statement, which is how to change the color of the links within your document:

```
document.link = "red"
```

This DOM statement changes the color of the links within your page to the named color, red. Simple. The value "red" is associated with the "link" property, which is valid for this "document", which is an object. All DOM statements begin with an object, which is followed by a property of that object. The property of the object is then followed by the value, which in this case was a color. All objects and methods are separated from their properties by a period. All values are separated from their properties by an equals sign and are enclosed within double quotes. This convention is universal to all DOM statements, with zero exceptions. It is this strict adherence to syntactical rules that makes DOM so easy and versatile to use.

Where you apply your DOM statement is as important as the statement itself. In using CSS with HTML, you've seen examples of this. Applying the attributes for a color to the BODY element resulted in the color being rendered for the entire document. Applying the same color to one individual element or groups of page elements resulted in only those elements being colored. It is the same in DOM, but with a few exceptions.

In DOM, every statement references the properties of a page element or the rules of a style sheet, which are the properties of an object within your page. Take the previous example of coloring all the links within the page with the color red. This is a global statement because it is applied to the "document" object without specifying any other object or property. The sequence in which you state your DOM instructions is very important in that it defines where your value will be applied. The placement of your values and properties is logical and ordered. Take the color property, for instance. Stating it with the background property will color the background. Stating it with the link property will color the link.

In your use of DOM, you'll see that the wording you use is of paramount importance. The individual wording obviously tells the browser what changes or modifications to make and when. Most DOM statements begin with the "document" keyword, which indicates that the following instructions are to be carried out within the current document. An optional window name may be stated before the "document" keyword to indicate that the instructions are to be carried out in a different window or frame of that name.

To make the implementation of DOM within your pages logical and ordered, and thus easy to use, a hierarchical approach is taken in the construction of your DOM statement. That is, when the browser reads your page, it constructs a tree consisting of the individual HTML page elements, attributes, and values stated within it. Elements are higher within the tree than are attributes, and attributes are higher within the tree than are the values of that attribute. Page elements appearing at the top of the HTML document are higher within the tree than are those preceding it. The stated portions of the HTML document must obviously be valid, and the DOM statements you specify must fit within this tree.

# Understanding the Document Statement Hierarchy

In working with objects, it is important to know and understand the cascading effect in which your DOM statements will be applied. The most basic DOM statement consists of three statements: an object and a property of that object, followed by the value that is to be changed. The browser, when reading an HTML document, constructs a hierarchy of cascading objects, each being referenced by the object that is higher in the hierarchical tree. Understanding this hierarchical approach is crucial to building valid, functional DOM statements. Consider the following sample code, which was stated on a previous page:

```
document.body.alink = "red"
```

When the browser reads this statement, it looks in the hierarchical tree it has built for the document. If it finds a match, it applies the value, which in this case is a red colored active link. The thing to understand is that the DOM statement must reflect the components of the object tree that the browser has built when it read the document. There are a few simple rules to help you understand this tree and how it is built:

1. The "document" object is almost always the highest on the tree, since the "document" contains everything else within the web page.

2. The tree is built in source code order. That is, the objects that are higher in the document source code are the highest on the tree.

3. HTML page elements are higher in the tree than are the attributes of that element.

4. HTML attributes are higher in the tree than are the values of that attribute.

5. HTML elements such as BODY that encompass the entire rendered portion of the document are higher on the tree. This includes the HTML, and perhaps a SPAN tag, if it is encompassing the entire BODY portion of the document.

6. Deeply nested tags such as tables within tables are the lowest on the tree.

7. CSS rules are considered to be low on the tree, since they are accessed with the "style" object, which is at least four graduations down from the top of the tree. Keeping these rules in mind, consider the following example:

```
document.all.elementID.style.bgColor = "blue"
```

In reading this statement, your eyes have passed over the hierarchical tree, from top to bottom. The highest on the tree is the "document" object, since the "document" is the container for everything else on the tree. The second from the top is the "all" object. Next comes the elementID, which you'll learn about in a later section of this chapter. Next is the "style" object. Beneath that is the bgColor property. Following the property is the value in quotes, "blue". Can you work out what this statement changes? It changes the background color of the element that has been assigned the elementID (through the use of the ID or CLASS attributes; don't worry, we'll get to that soon).

This method of working down from the top of the hierarchical document tree is the way DOM accesses the objects which the browser has built into the tree itself. Deeply nested objects are accessed through very long (sometimes ridiculously long) statements. The general rule is that if the statement is more than six or seven components long, it is time to think about restructuring your HTML document into something more streamlined.

# The ID and CLASS Selectors and a DOM Statement

Using CSS style rules within your document greatly reduces the complexity and size of your finished product while providing a large array of effects and user customization. CSS style rules are used in some way within almost all of today's Internet documents. Recognizing this widespread use, the makers of the Document Object Model have provided a means to change or set these style rules on the fly. There is a DOM statement to fit almost every CSS rule that has been created. The gateway to these CSS rules is the "style" object implemented within Internet Explorer. It uses the HTML ID and CLASS attributes to know where to apply the changes you desire. Used with event handlers, you may change or set every aspect of your document. Colors, fonts, sizes, alignment, margins, and just about everything you can imagine can be changed on the fly according to user action. While these concepts will be addressed in a later lesson, the point at which to begin is simply learning to assign the action to a very specific place.

To specify where the actions are to be placed, a unique ID or CLASS attribute must be stated. This indicates to the browser that the tag the attribute is stated within is unique within the document. CSS rules may then be assigned accordingly.

As in HTML and CSS, in order to apply a DOM statement to a specific page element, you would use the ID or CLASS element selector. The selector is stated as part of the DOM statement, between the object and the object property, as in the following example:

```
document.all.banner.style.bgColor = "red"
```

This sample bit of code assigns a value of red to the page element that has been assigned the ID or CLASS identification of "banner". You would of course use a value that has something in common with the page element to which you are applying the value. For example, assigning a color value to an element whose only definitive property is its border width just doesn't make sense. Common sense is applicable at all times.

You'll use this method of assigning a value to a specific ID or CLASS identifier often in your continuing use of the DOM specifications. Using the various properties available from the aforementioned "style" object, you'll be able to access and change all of the rules that have been set using the CSS specifications.

# Accessing CSS Rules via DOM

Now that you've covered the use of ID and CLASS selectors with DOM, it is time to cover the implementation. To access the CSS rules within a document, DOM has provided the "style" object. Stated with an ID or CLASS selector, the style object is the link between the higher "all" object and the property you wish to change. There are about 400 different properties available to be changed within every individual document you'll be working with. There is a bewildering amount of different values you may assign to these properties.

As you've already learned, assigning a CSS rule to a block of text is a streamlined and efficient use of both your bandwidth and your time. In order to access the CSS rules through the DOM specifications, you would use the "style" object and its long list of available properties. Consider the following example of the syntax involved in accessing your CSS rules through the Document Object Model:

```
document.all.elementID.style.CSSproperty = "value"
```

Through the use of the "document.all" and "style" objects, every rule and value available from the Cascading Style Sheet specifications may be set or changed. Using the ID or CLASS selector, you can assign a CSS rule to be changed or set for an individual page element or a block of page elements. The elementID is the ID or CLASS selector name that you have assigned to that page element. The CSSproperty is the HTML attribute that you would like to set or change.

Although the "style" part of the aforementioned statement is itself an object, it is also a property. That is, it is a property of the "document.all" group of objects. This somewhat confusing nomenclature will become clear to you as we progress through the use of the Document Object Model.

The values you specify using the aforementioned DOM properties will override any previously existing CSS rules assigned with the STYLE attribute, the STYLE tag, or style rules from an external style sheet. For example, the following entry within an external style sheet will be applied when the document is loading:

```
table1 {color: "lightpink"};
```

Then, through the use of an onLoad event handler within the BODY element, the color of the text within the table1 container may be changed with the following statement when the document has completed loading:

```
<BODY onLoad="document.all.table1.style.color = darkpink">
```

You can see that the initial CSS rule stated within the external style sheet is overridden. This is applicable to all style rules, no exceptions. Any event handler or combinations of event handlers may be used, as well as any valid DOM statement.

# Using DOM Arrays

Within the DOM Language specifications are about 16 arrays that are used to access the properties of the object within the HTML document you are working with. Arrays are called Collections by some because they collect information about the objects within the document being worked with. The 16 arrays we'll be working with are as follows:

1.  all[ ] – Contains references to all the items within the page

2.  anchors[ ] – Contains a reference to every instance of the anchor tag within the document

3. applets[ ] – Contains a reference to every instance of the APPLET tag within the document

4. classes[ ] – Contains a reference to every instance of the CLASS attribute within the document

5. children[ ] – Contains a reference to every child of a parent container within the document

6. embeds[ ] – Contains a reference to every instance of the EMBED tag within the document

7. filters[ ] – Contains a reference to every instance of the CSS FILTER attribute within the document

8. forms[ ] – Contains a reference to every instance of a FORM element within the document

9. frames[ ] – Contains a reference to every frame within the document

10. ids[ ] – Contains a reference to every instance of the ID attribute within the document

11. images[ ] – Contains a reference to every image included in the document through the use of an IMG tag

12. links[ ] – Contains a reference to every instance of the anchor tag within the document

13. plugins[ ] – Contains a reference to every plug-in that is valid and operating for the document

14. scripts[ ] – Contains a reference to every instance of the SCRIPT tag within the document

15. stylesheets[ ] – Contains a reference to every instance a style rule is used within the document

16. tags[ ] – Contains a reference to every valid HTML tag within the document

You can see from the preceding array listing that the contents of the arrays can be deduced just by their names – the anchors[ ] array contains all of the anchors defined by the <A> tag within the document, for example. Using arrays only, you can access all of the elements within the HTML document. There is even an "all[ ]" array, which contains every single element read by the browser. Accessing the content of any array is fairly simple and logical.

Every item within the array is represented by a number that represents its order within the array. Think of the array as a list of items, like a shopping list. Now number the list starting at the top. Since the number 0 is considered a whole number by most programming languages (including DOM), start your numbering at zero. The array items, then, can be accessed by citing the number, the index number, that contains the page item you wish to act upon.

## Accessing the Array Items

Now that you know how the items within an array are ordered (indexed), we can now move on to how you actually access the contents of an array. Consider the following example:

```
window.document.anchors[3].style.color="red"
```

The preceding example shows the change of color for the fourth instance of an anchor within the document to the named color, red. The window statement is optional, and if it is left out of the statement, the browser assumes the command is to be performed within the current window. Notice that the number within the square brackets is the number three yet is referencing the fourth instance of an anchor. This is because the arrays are zero based. That is, the numbering starts and includes the number 0. All of the arrays you'll be working with for most languages work in this way, so get used to it now.

In the preceding list of arrays, you can see that using the arrays compiled by the DOM engine can be a very useful way to achieve your desired effect. The array items can be used to change the appearance of your page on the fly, according to user input. In the use of the arrays, it is not only appearance that can be affected – you can also use the arrays as powerful reporting tools. Consider the plugins[ ] array. It contains a list of all of the plug-ins that can be used by the browser, that is, all the plug-ins your users have installed to their browser. You may devise a script that checks the list to determine if the required plug-in is installed, or you can print the list to the screen. Printing the list to the screen is fairly simple to do; all that is required is a JavaScript document.write statement, which you'll find in the JavaScript Language Reference and within the JavaScript Tutorial.

# Summary

In this chapter, we learned the use of the Document Object Model – referred to as DOM or the DOM – and applied it to real-world situations. Using DOM as part of your page's executable code is almost a necessity. There aren't many ways of rendering a page of any complexity without using DOM on some level.

## Summary

# CHAPTER 6

# Practical JavaScript Concepts and Projects

This chapter looks at some useful JavaScript concepts and projects that span everything from menus to links, coloring, and positioning concerns. I've provided about 50 individual code examples with detailed descriptions for each. Some are a little complicated, but for these, I've just included more explanations.

I tried to keep the skill level as an increasing progression – one leads to another. We'll be using these essential skills in the chapters to come. Enjoy.

## Turning Visibility On and Off

You've no doubt run into a situation whereby you've clicked an action object and had other options, such as links or images, made visible on the page. This is accomplished via the use of the DOM style method of the document object. In this example, the hidden attribute is simply switched from "hidden" to "visible" when the input button is clicked. The action is an HTML onClick event handler, and it is shown how to change this property on two input buttons, given in Listing 6-1.

***Listing 6-1.*** Toggling the visible and hidden page elements

```
<html>
<body>
<p id="x">This is text. This is text. This is text.</p>
<input type="button" value="Hide text" onclick="document.
getElementById('x').style.visibility='hidden'">
```

73

T. Valentine, *Database-Driven Web Development*, https://doi.org/10.1007/978-1-4842-9792-6_6

```
<input type="button" value="Show text" onclick="document.
getElementById('x').style.visibility='visible'">
</body>
</html>
```

It should be mentioned that older browsers may need you to adjust your thinking a little to accommodate them. If you notice, the "x" identifier has been merely stated in the onClick declaration – it has no action other than to identify that piece of the document as a unique part. In the P element above it, the id attribute is set to x before the DOM statement is applied. The standard bubbling order rules apply, so the x identifier has to be declared before the DOM statement. Otherwise, you'll get an error that it can't locate the document element that you're referring to (x).

# Change the Background Color of an Element

The following chunk of code shows how to make changes to the background color of a few table elements. In this example, the action is applied only to the TD element of the table that it is declared within. You can apply this method to any page element that DOM allows access to, including making document-wide changes through altering the values of attributes of the BODY element.

These methods can be used in one page element or in sweeping changes that you can accomplish through the use of CSS rules. Simply alter the DOM statement stated in the JavaScript within the script elements given in the head of the document accordingly.

*Listing 6-2.* Changing colors dynamically

```
<html>
<head>
<script type="text/javascript">
function bgChange(bg) {
      document.body.style.background=bg;
}
</script>
</head>
<body>
<b>Mouse over the squares and the background color will change</b>
```

```
<table width="300" height="100">
 <tr>
  <td onmouseover="bgChange('red')"
      onmouseout="bgChange('transparent')"
      bgcolor="red">
  </td>
  <td onmouseover="bgChange('blue')"
      onmouseout="bgChange('transparent')"
      bgcolor="blue">
  </td>
  <td onmouseover="bgChange('green')"
      onmouseout="bgChange('transparent')"
      bgcolor="green">
  </td>
 </tr>
</table>
</body>
</html>
```

Some things that you might want to play around with are changing which events fire the changes stated in the DOM statement, what properties are altered, and if you want to go a bit further and assign a variable loaded with information that is decided upon by other functions such as according to stored user preference.

To do this, change from using a literal value as the argument passed to the bgChange() function. For example, use a variable name instead of the word "green" – the actual color to be applied can be decided upon in another function and is contained as the data of the variable. You may use named colors, hex colors, or RGB colors as the method of defining what color is to be applied.

# An onLoad Event Trigger

Learning to use an onLoad event handler is great. Through the use of this simple event handler, you can time actions to coincide with subtle things such as starting an action when the page element is finished loading and is displayed – applying a CSS rule when a large image has finished downloading, for example.

Try downloading a large file such as an audio or video file. Change the border property of a table to 1 with a bgcolor="red" statement and a border will be displayed around the object that is 1 pixel wide, colored red, when the file is finished loading into the page. Put the instructions in a script in the head of the document and state the JavaScript function within the body of the document as that to be processed when the onLoad event is triggered.

Listing 6-3 uses the onLoad event in the BODY element to display an alert box with the text given when the entire document is finished loading. You don't have to apply this rule in terms of document-wide alterations – the onLoad event can be triggered in any HTML element and applied when the element is finished loading by the browser.

***Listing 6-3.*** Using the onLoad() event handler

```html
<html>
<head>
<script type="text/javascript">
function myMessage() {
alert("This message was triggered from the onLoad event");
}
</script>
</head>
<body onload="myMessage()">
</body>
</html>
```

You can accomplish quite a bit of creative actions using this simple event. Try mixing this event with its opposite, the onUnload event handler. onUnload is very handy to write user preferences or any generated data to a cookie when the page is closed, I've found. You can then use the data contained within the cookie and apply it to the next page by applying it using the onLoad function in the next page.

# Use "this" to Change Colors

This is a very simple way to achieve some impressive results. The DOM directive is triggered with a simple onClick event, changing the original color of the Click Me! Text to red. You may use a named color, hex color, or RGB color.

The this directive can be very powerful when used in a unique position. However, you wouldn't want to change many items in a document with this approach. It is inefficient on a large scale and isn't the best approach to solving the problem of document-wide or even selective area alterations.

***Listing 6-4.*** Using the this directive

```
<html>
<body>
<h1 onclick="this.style.color='red'">Click Me!</h1>
</body>
</html>
```

You can apply this technique to any properly formed container in any given document, since HTML version 3.2. This functionality is widespread, so it will be included in every version of HTML (and thus DOM) for the foreseeable future.

# Switching Images on the Fly

Switching images is fairly simple as long as you realize a couple of things: you must preload the image data that you want to switch to into a variable, and if you want to change the image back, you have to load the original image data into a variable of its own. You accomplish through the use of the src attribute of the document object. Examine the example in Listing 6-5.

***Listing 6-5.*** Manipulating images

```
<html>
<body>
<img id="image" src="image1.gif" width="160" height="120">
<script type="text/javascript">
document.getElementById("image").src="image2.jpg";
</script>
<p>The original image was image1.gif The script changed it to
image2.jpg</p>
</body>
</html>
```

You can place the JavaScript function that accomplishes this action in any place within the document. However, older browsers require that you place the function in a section of the document that is parsed before the location of the image is stated to be changed. You can use a JavaScript function within the opening and closing SCRIPT elements, or you can use a javascript: parameter of any given legal element within the HTML specifications.

To change the image back to the original image, you must use the same src attribute of the document object to do so – simply change the URL of the image file. The browser will load the data and store it until it is triggered with the event handler of your choice.

In the preceding example, we used two variables to store and retrieve the image data. It is entirely possible, and in some cases, desirable, to use one array rather than many variables. Simply declare the array, assign the src attribute in the exact way given previously, but use an arrayName[count]= assignment instead of a simple variable declaration.

You would use this technique if you need to change many different images in many different portions of the document, at different times. You should use variables if you wish to change many images that are the same at the same time – the image data stored in the variable can be used repeatedly.

# Change HTML Code Using innerHTML

The innerHTML attribute is sometimes a little confusing in its use, I've found. For some reason, outerHTML seems to be the best choice for most people, but this isn't always the case – the proof for this is simply because the innerHTML attribute was included in the HTML specifications, not just the outerHTML attribute.

Use the id attribute to assign the JavaScript commands within the nameon() function to that individual page element. Call the name given as the value of the id attribute as the argument passed to the two functions we're using to accomplish our goals. We use two events to trigger two separate actions: onMouseOut and onMouseOver.

*Listing 6-6.* An exercise in innerHTML

```
<html>
<head>
<script type="text/javascript">
function nameon() {
```

```
document.getElementById('h2text').innerHTML="WELCOME!";
}
function nameout() {
document.getElementById('h2text').innerHTML="How are you today?";
}
</script>
</head>
<body>
<h2 id="h2text" onMouseOut="nameout()" onMouseOver="nameon()">Mouse over
this text!</h2>
</body>
</html>
```

This is especially useful if you have an action that must change as the user triggers an event. You don't have to stop with one command, remember, so you can load whatever functionality you'd like within the functions. The innerHTML attribute is used primarily as a text editing directive, but with a little forethought and creativity, you can assign DOM style sheet rules when the text is changed. Each set of text you'd like to include as the changed content can have its own style sheet rules applied to it.

# Change the Position of a Page Element

Before we get into the use of the style.position statement, you must understand how the two options of this statement differ. You would usually use them with ilayer elements to accomplish a drop-down menu. Each has its pros and cons, and each has a very particular way they must be used.

The first option is absolute. The absolute positioned document element is positioned according to a position the browser calculates in relation to the top left corner of the document. It is expressed in pixels. The element assigned to this positioning schema will stay in the position given even if the rest of the document resizes or shifts as the browser window is resized.

For example, if you absolutely positioned a centered table in your document and the user resized the window, that portion of the table that is absolutely referenced will stay where it is – the rest of the document will move. If you'd like to use this positioning technique, you must, for practical reasons, position your page justified left, valign=top.

This is because the document is positioned absolutely according to the top-left corner of the document. If the browser window is resized, the page doesn't move, and the absolutely positioned element will have the same referenced location in the document.

The relatively positioned page element is by far the most useful. It is usually applied as a position in a table. The position is referenced as a point positioned absolutely, but in reference to the upper left corner of the area of the document specified by the TD element. If the page is resized, the TD element will move, but the content attached to the upper left corner of that element will adjust as the TD element adjusts, keeping the structure of the table intact. A browser resize, then, will move the entire table including the relatively positioned portion given as content within the table.

***Listing 6-7.*** Positioning page elements

```
<html>
<head>
<script type="text/javascript">
function moveleft() {
document.getElementById('header').style.position="absolute";
document.getElementById('header').style.left="0";
}
function moveback() {
document.getElementById('header').style.position="relative";
}
</script>
</head>
<body>
<h1 id="header" onmouseover="moveleft()" onmouseout="moveback()">Mouse over
this text</h1>
</body>
</html>
```

Notice that the style.left attribute was stated as the second statement within the JavaScript function. This is the value, in pixels, that the browser will use to position the content. Notice also that you don't have to use the style.left attribute if you're positioning relatively.

# Using onMouseMove

onMouseMove is a document-wide event handler that applies to the BODY element only. You can use a javascript approach, but that is usually not a good thing, as it clutters up your BODY element with unneeded attributes. Use a JavaScript function in the head of the document and call it with the onMouseMove event handler as per usual.

***Listing 6-8.*** Using the onMouseMove event handler

```
<html>
<head>
<script type="text/javascript">
var i=1;
function moveright() {
document.getElementById('header').style.position="absolute";
document.getElementById('header').style.left=i;
i++;
}
</script>
</head>
<body onmousemove="moveright()">
<h1 id="header">Move the mouse over this page</h1>
</body>
</html>
```

Note that a variable loaded with a value was used as the parameter of the style.left attribute. This is just to show that a variable name can be used as the value. You may use other JavaScript functions within the rest of the document to calculate the value given in the variable. This will allow a limited sort of dynamic positioning while still receiving the benefits of the rules that govern the absolutely positioned document element.

# Using onLoad and onUnload

The load event handlers are great to work with. There are many different ways you can use them, and all are very useful and easy to implement. The two JavaScript functions used in the example are fairly basic, although the first function, starttimer(), uses four DOM statements and two JavaScript object activations.

***Listing 6-9.*** Using the onLoad and onUnload event handlers

```html
<html>
<head>
<script type="text/javascript">
var i=10
function starttimer() {
document.getElementById('h_one').style.position="relative";
document.getElementById('h_one').style.left=+i;
document.getElementById('h_two').style.position="relative";
document.getElementById('h_two').style.top=+i;
i++;
}
</script>
</head>
<body onLoad="starttimer()" onUnload="stoptimer()">
<h1 id="h_one">Header one</h1>
<h1 id="h_two">Header two</h1>
</body>
</html>
```

The JavaScript functions we've stated are relatively positioned. The value of this relatively positioned portion of the document is given in the i variable. Note that the increment operand (+) is used with the variable name. This increments the numeric value within the variable by one, changing the position of said page element.

It is extremely handy to be able to carry data from one page to the next without first sending that data to the web server to be stored, processed, and re-served for the next page. Using the onUnload event handler, you are able to attach a series of nested commands that allow you to store data such as user preferences in a cookie on the user machine and load from that cookie to format the next page on the fly through the use of the onLoad event handler.

# Making Text Bigger

Applying a textual formatting application is very easy. Simply use any CSS rule that has been included in the DOM specifications. In this case, we're altering the sizing of text. We'll take it a step further and introduce a maximum text size as well.

***Listing 6-10.*** Changing text size properties

```
<html>
<head>
<script type="text/javascript">
txtsize=0;
maxsize=100;
function writemsg() {
      if (txtsize<maxsize) {
            document.getElementById('msg').style.fontSize=txtsize;
            txtsize++;
      }
}
</script>
</head>
<body onload="writemsg()">
<p id="msg">This is the text that will become bigger</p>
</body>
</html>
```

The style.fontSize attribute is used to change the size of the text. There are many style rules that can be used in this exact same location in this exact way to change many different textual formatting options. However, you are not limited to applying only one textual formatting option per function – you may also apply groups of rules to construct the look and feel you're thinking of.

# Change the Background Color of an "input" Field

This option can easily be applied as the page loads or according to user selection. We use the style.background statement to change the color. The color can be stated as a named color, hex color, or RGB color.

*Listing 6-11.* Changing the color of an INPUT field

```
<html>
<head>
<script type="text/javascript">
function changeColor(color) {
      document.getElementById('x').style.background=color;
}
</script>
</head>
<body>
<p>Mouse over the three table cells, and the input field will change its
background color</p>
<table width="100%">
<tr>
      <td bgcolor="red" onmouseover="changeColor('red')"></td>
      <td bgcolor="blue" onmouseover="changeColor('blue')"></td>
      <td bgcolor="green" onmouseover="changeColor('green')"></td>
</tr>
</table>
<form>
<input id="x" type="text" value="Mouse over the colors" size="20">
</form>
</body>
</html>
```

Be sure to use an appropriate id attribute on the input field you want to apply changes to. The arguments passed to the changeColor() function are stated in a static way as named colors but can also be decided upon with other functions by replacing the named color with a variable. The value of the value can then be decided by other functions within the page.

# Change the Text Color of an "input" Field

A simple way to change the text within an input field is by using the oft-used style.color statement. It can be changed according to one option or many options. It is also entirely possible to make these decisions on what color to change to a part of other JavaScript functions.

The coloring methods used are named colors, hex colors, or RGB colors. You may mix the three at any given point in the logical progression of the script.

*Listing 6-12.* Changing the text color of an INPUT field

```html
<html>
<head>
<script type="text/javascript">
function changeColor(color) {
      document.getElementById('x').style.color=color;
}
</script>
</head>
<body>
<p>Mouse over the three colored table cells. The text will change
color. </p>
<table width="100%">
<tr>
      <td bgcolor="red" onmouseover="changeColor('red')"> </td>
      <td bgcolor="blue" onmouseover="changeColor('blue')"> </td>
      <td bgcolor="green" onmouseover="changeColor('green')"> </td>
</tr>
</table>
<form>
<input id="x" type="text" value="Mouse over the colors" size="20">
</form>
</body>
</html>
```

Note that this method of changing textual formatting can be applied to anywhere within the document using any valid DOM reflection of a CSS rule.

# Change the Background Image of an "input" Field

There are many websites that use this small but powerful chunk of functionality. The Internet is based on look and feel, so it is obviously very common to have to work with a large amount of display options. The easiest to understand is simply changing the background image used in a text input field.

We use a preloader to fetch the image data that is going to be displayed. The src attribute of the document object is used to tell the browser the location of the file. Upon the page loading, the data for the image is fetched and stored and is immediately available to the entire page. It should be noted that if you wish to switch the displayed image back to the original image, you would have to use another src attribute statement to fetch the original image data and store it. You may then provide to have the image switched back according to your requirements.

***Listing 6-13.*** Working with an image as the background

```
<html>
<head>
<script type="text/javascript">
function bgChange(bg) {
      document.getElementById('x').style.background="url(" + bg + ")";
}
</script>
</head>
<body>
<p>Mouse over these images. The input field will get a new background
image.</p>
<table width="300" height="100">
<tr>
      <td onmouseover="bgChange('image1.jpg')" background="image2.jpg"></td>
      <td onmouseover="bgChange('image2.jpg')" background="image1.jpg"></td>
</tr>
</table>
<form>
```

```
<input id="x" type="text" value="Mouse over the images" size="20">
</form>
</body>
</html>
```

Use a simple id attribute to uniquely identify the page element to apply the change to. This id is used as the argument of the getElementById object. We then use a style. background attribute to select from the many style sheet options available and apply the new value when the onMouseOver event is triggered. You may use a relative or absolute URL for the location of the image file, and the image format can be any that the browser supports, in this case, a .jpg.

# Select All of the Check Boxes in a Form

This is a very useful procedure to implement and is fairly simple to understand. In working with forms, you'll no doubt need to include this in at least one page if you have a large amount of options to select or if you work with long lists. An example of this functionality is the Yahoo Mail option to select all email messages for deletion or moving. The checked=true value is used to check all of the check boxes within that one form. It is important to realize that this will work only if you're using a single form (of any size). If you have more than one form to submit on the same page with this functionality, you'll have to provide an entirely separate checked=true statement within a different function.

***Listing 6-14.*** Selecting all check boxes in an HTML form

```
<html>
<head>
<script type="text/javascript">
function makeCheck(thisForm) {
    for (i = 0; i < thisForm.option.length; i++) {
        thisForm.option[i].checked=true;
    }
}
function makeUncheck(thisForm) {
    for (i = 0; i < thisForm.option.length; i++) {
```

```
            thisForm.option[i].checked=false;
    }
}
</script>
</head>
<body>
<form name="form">
<input type="button" value="Check" onclick="makeCheck(this.form)">
<input type="button" value="Uncheck" onclick="makeUncheck(this.form)">
<input type="checkbox" name="option">CheckBox1<br>
<input type="checkbox" name="option"> CheckBox2<br>
<input type="checkbox" name="option"> CheckBox3<br>
<input type="checkbox" name="option"> CheckBox4
</form>
</body>
</html>
```

You may use a type=submit button to check all boxes and submit at the same time if
you like. This is usually used in the case of having trained employees who are using the
form over many times on an Intranet or private Internet page. They know that the form
will be submitted with all boxes being checked. An Internet page that the user visits only
once shouldn't have this functionality, as the user may not completely understand what
just happened simply because they've never used that particular form before.

# Select the Background Color of a Submit Button

Internet pages are a visual medium and being such should look as good as possible. The
default gray color of a Submit button sometimes just will not do, so you're now able to
change this color to any within the normal palette of millions of colors. You can specify a
permanent color within CSS rules in the head of the document or change it dynamically
or according to user input.

You may use any coloring method such as named colors, hex colors, or RGB
colors. We use the style.color attribute to apply the color change and call it with an
onMouseOver event. Notice that the color is given as a static named color. You may

substitute this static value with a JavaScript variable or array index value. In this way, the value (the color) may be decided upon by a different JavaScript function and applied exactly as it would be if you're stating a static value.

***Listing 6-15.*** Changing the background color of an INPUT element

```
<html>
<head>
<script type="text/javascript">
function changeColor(color) {
    document.getElementById('x').style.background=color;
}
</script>
</head>
<body>
<p>Mouse over the three colored table cells. The background color will
change:</p>
<table width="100%">
<tr>
    <td bgcolor="red" onmouseover="changeColor('red')"></td>
    <td bgcolor="blue" onmouseover="changeColor('blue')"></td>
    <td bgcolor="green" onmouseover="changeColor('green')"></td>
</tr>
</table>
<form>
<input id="x" type="button" value="Mouse over the colors">
</form>
</body>
</html>
```

Use an id attribute within the page element you're committing the changes to. This should be reflected as the argument passed to the getElementById object. The new color is applied when the onMouseOver event is triggered.

# Change the Text Color of a Submit Button

The coloring of text is extremely important, as it is the part of the page that conveys the most information and thus effect on your users. We use the style.color attribute to assign a new color and an onMouseOver event to trigger the assignment. The new color value is a static named color in this example, but it doesn't always have to be – you can substitute the static value with a variable name and use a different function to arrive at the color value your users prefer, for example.

The coloring method may be named colors, hex colors, or RGB colors. You aren't limited to applying only a text color change. You may also apply any formatting options available via the DOM reflection of every CSS rule. These rules are part of the style attribute, and there are many of them. Simply provide another legal style directive on another line within the JavaScript function in the head of the document.

***Listing 6-16.*** Changing the text color of an HTML INPUT element

```
<html>
<head>
<script type="text/javascript">
function changeColor(color) {
    document.getElementById('x').style.color=color;
}
</script>
</head>
<body>
<p>Mouse over the three table cells. The text color will change:</p>
<table width="100%">
<tr>
    <td bgcolor="red" onmouseover="changeColor('red')"></td>
    <td bgcolor="blue" onmouseover="changeColor('blue')"></td>
    <td bgcolor="green" onmouseover="changeColor('green')"></td>
</tr>
</table>
<form>
<input id="x" type="button" value="Mouse over the colors">
```

```
</form>
</body>
</html>
```

It should be noted that if you would like to change back to the original color, a different JavaScript function would have to be created to do this. You would usually trigger the change with an onMouseOut event handler that calls this new function.

# Insert a Background Image on a Button

Providing a background image as that to display as the Submit button is always a good idea. The flat default gray-colored button just isn't very nice to look at. Use any size image for your button – the browser will automatically size the button accordingly. Keep it to a practical size, of course.

We use the style.background attribute to adjust the image to be used. The URL to the file may be given as absolute or relative and can be any image format the browser supports. An onMouseOver event is used to trigger the execution of the JavaScript function given in the head of the document.

***Listing 6-17.*** Changing the background image of an HTML INPUT element

```
<html>
<head>
<script type="text/javascript">
function bgChange(bg) {
     document.getElementById('x').style.background="url(" + bg + ")";
}
</script>
</head>
<body>
<p>Mouse over these images. The button will get a new background image.</p>
<table width="300" height="100">
<tr>
     <td onmouseover="bgChange('image1.jpg')" background="image1.
     jpg"></td>
```

```
    <td onmouseover="bgChange('image2.jpg')" background="image
2.jpg"></td>
</tr>
</table>
<form>
<input id="x" type="button" value="Mouse over the images">
</form>
</body>
</html>
```

Adding a bit of customization can be fun. One idea for this is to change the image as the button is clicked. You would need to create a different JavaScript function within the head of the document with the exact same directions; just change the file name. Use an onMouseDown event to change to the down image you'd like to use and an onMouseUp event to change the image back as the up image.

# Change the Background Color of a Drop-Down List

A drop-down list is usually colored with a simple white background. You can change this using the style.background attribute to any color within the normal range available (millions of colors). The color value may be stated as a named color, hex color, or RGB color.

We use the style.background attribute in a JavaScript function within the head of the document. This function is triggered with an onMouseOver event, and the new color is applied.

***Listing 6-18.*** Working with lists

```
<html>
<head>
<script type="text/javascript">
function changeColor(color) {
     formname.elements[0].style.background=color;
}
</script>
</head>
```

```
<body>
<p>Mouse over the three table cells. The option list will change color:</p>
<table width="100%">
<tr>
     <td bgcolor="red" onmouseover="changeColor('red')"> </td>
     <td bgcolor="blue" onmouseover="changeColor('blue')"> </td>
     <td bgcolor="green" onmouseover="changeColor('green')"> </td>
</tr>
</table>
<form name="formname">
<select>
     <option>Mouse over the colored table cells</option>
     <option>Mouse over the colored table cells</option>
     <option>Mouse over the colored table cells</option>
     <option>Mouse over the colored table cells</option>
</select>
</form>
</body>
</html>
```

Notice that we stated the color to be used as a named color. This appears as the argument that is passed to the changeColor() function created in the head of the document. In this example, we used the form name with the elements[0] collection to state which page element is to be used. You may use a document.getElementById(formname) statement if you're more comfortable with that.

# Change the Text Color of a Drop-Down List

Sometimes, the default text color – black – just doesn't work with your page. You can easily change this color upon page loading or dynamically according to user preferences. We use a style.color statement to access and apply the new color to the page element that is specified with the name= attribute.

We use an onMouseOver event to trigger the JavaScript function that is given in the head of the document. The actual color value stated is a named color and is given as the argument passed to the JavaScript function that was created, in this case, changeColor(). The coloring method used may be named colors, hex colors, or RGB colors.

***Listing 6-19.*** Changing the text color of an HTML INPUT element

```html
<html>
<head>
<script type="text/javascript">
function changeColor(color) {
     thisform.elements[0].style.color=color;
}
</script>
</head>
<body>
<p>Mouse over the three table cells. The option list text will change
color:</p>
<table width="100%">
<tr>
     <td bgcolor="red" onmouseover="changeColor('red')"> </td>
     <td bgcolor="blue" onmouseover="changeColor('blue')"> </td>
     <td bgcolor="green" onmouseover="changeColor('green')"> </td>
</tr>
</table>
<form name="thisform">
<select>
     <option>Mouse over the colored table cells</option>
     <option>Mouse over the colored table cells</option>
     <option>Mouse over the colored table cells</option>
     <option>Mouse over the colored table cells</option>
</select>
</form>
</body>
</html>
```

Notice that I didn't give name= or value= values in the option elements in the example. This is because the server-side script doesn't need them if your form name= attribute is stated. All of the option elements will be treated as part of the form being submitted. It should be noted, though, that you would have to state name= and value= attributes if you're using more than one form within a single page. This is a browser requirement, not a server-side scripting issue.

# Change the Background Color of a Textarea Element

Textarea spaces are usually fairly large, so they affect the appearance of your page in a big way. Coloring them can be a great way to add a unique impression upon your visitors. We use the style.background attribute to alter this. You may have the color change as the default color that is applied as the page loads or at any time according to user action.

We use an onMouseOver event to trigger the JavaScript function that is given in the head of the document. The coloring method may be stated as a named color, hex color, or RGB color.

***Listing 6-20.*** Changing the background color of an HTML TEXTAREA element

```
<html>
<head>
<script type="text/javascript">
function newColor(color) {
      document.getElementById('x').style.background=color;
}
</script>
</head>
<body>
<p>Mouse over the three table cells. The textarea background will change
color:</p>
<table width="100%">
<tr>
      <td bgcolor="red" onmouseover="newColor('red')"></td>
      <td bgcolor="blue" onmouseover="newColor('blue')"></td>
      <td bgcolor="green" onmouseover="newColor('green')"></td>
```

95

```
</tr>
</table>
<form>
<textarea id="x" rows="5" cols="20"></textarea>
</form>
</body>
</html>
```

The new background color is stated as the argument passed to the newColor() function given in the JavaScript function stated in the head of the document. You may use a variable or array item as the value. In this way, the color to be applied can be decided by scripted action, such as per-user preference selection.

# Insert a Background Image into a Textarea Element

Inserting a background image into your TEXTAREA is an effective way to brand your site with a unique look and feel. Use any image format supported by the browser. The style.background=url attribute is used to give the location of the file and may be an absolute or relative URL.

The style.background attribute acts like the background=url attribute you might use with the BODY element. The image is displayed at its actual size, and any overlapping areas aren't shown if the textarea is smaller than the image. If the textarea element is larger than the image, it will be repeated (tiled).

*Listing 6-21.* Inserting an image into an HTML TEXTAREA element

```
<html>
<head>
<script type="text/javascript">
function bgChange(bg) {
     document.getElementById('x').style.background="url(" + bg + ")";
}
</script>
</head>
<body>
<p>Mouse over the images. The textarea will get a background image.</p>
```

```
<table width="300" height="100">
<tr>
    <td onmouseover="bgChange('image1.jpg')" background="image1.jpg"></td>
    <td onmouseover="bgChange('image2.jpg')" background="image2.jpg"></td>
</tr>
</table>
<form>
<textarea id="x" rows="5" cols="20"></textarea>
</form>
</body>
</html>
```

I've seen a few sites that use the background image as an informative indicator to the user. It is entirely possible to count the number of characters being typed in the TEXTAREA and change the image that is displayed according to these counted values. A progress bar can be displayed as the background image as the user types, giving them the idea of how much more characters they have to add if you've specified a minimum or the amount of characters they have left if you've specified a maximum.

# Preload and Store an Image

Image preloading is an essential skill that you'll use repeatedly. Consider this: you have loaded your page and have a menu system that uses images that change as the mouse floats over them. Once the page is loaded, the user does so, but there is a lag between the mouse passing over that area and the new image being displayed. This is because the browser has to fetch the new image and display it. This lag can be eliminated if you preload the image into a variable as the page loads and trigger its display as the mouse floats over it. The process is essentially immediate and is a great effect.

*Listing 6-22.* Preload and store images

```
<html>
<head>
<script type="text/javascript">
img2=new Image();
img2.src="image1.gif";
```

```
function changeImage() {
     document.getElementById('myImage').src=img2.src;
}
</script>
</head>
<body>
<p>When you mouse over the image, a new image will appear.</p>
<img id="myImage" onmouseover="changeImage()" width="160" height="120"
src="image2.jpg">
</body>
</html>
```

We use an onMouseOver event to trigger the JavaScript function that is stated in the head of the document. The original image is displayed until the mouse floats over it. The new image is then displayed. Note that if you'd like to change back to the original image, you'd have to provide a different function name with the original file name and trigger it with an onMouseOut event.

# Changing the Size of an Image

It is entirely possible to change the size of an image. You may apply the changes to the same image or download a new image and display that, resized. We use the getElementById() method to access the data associated with that image, in this case, the image dimensions. The browser can be made to display an image in dimensions that aren't the actual size of the image. Because of this, it is possible to change the image dimensions dynamically.

*Listing 6-23.*  Changing the size of an image

```
<html>
<head>
<script type="text/javascript">
function moveover() {
     document.getElementById('image').width="200";
     document.getElementById('image').height="360";
}
```

```
function moveback() {
      document.getElementById('image').width="100";
      document.getElementById('image').height="180";
}
</script>
</head>
<body>
<b>Mouse over the image:</b><br />
<img id="image" src="bulbon.gif" onmouseover="moveover()"
onmouseout="moveback()">
</body>
</html>
```

A few things have to be considered if you're going to resize images. The first is simple page layout. If you use a table that contains the image to be resized, you'd alter the entire table upon the resize. Most of the time, this isn't what you want, so it is sometimes prudent to account for the new image dimensions. Within the TD element of the table, state the size of the TD area as the size of the largest image dimension. This way, the table isn't altered with an oversized image and the page looks as you intended.

# Changing the Source of an Image

You might have to alter the location of the image being displayed in that space on the page you're working with. You would do this with an src attribute declaration. The page element is accessed with the getElementById() method, and the image is changed. The image may be a different image or a duplicate image that is simply located elsewhere.

***Listing 6-24.*** Changing the source image to be used

```
<html>
<head>
<script type="text/javascript">
function moveover() {
      document.getElementById('image').src="imageon.gif";
}
function moveback() {
```

```
        document.getElementById('image').src="imageoff.gif";
}
</script>
</head>
<body>
<img id="image" src="imageoff.gif" onmouseover="moveover()"
onmouseout="moveback">
</body>
</html>
```

We used an onMouseOver event to trigger the first change and an onMouseOut event to change back to the original image. This is advantageous when you're working with images that must necessarily be located in different directories on even different servers. The URL may be stated as absolute or relative, according to needs. If you're changing servers, be sure to use the absolute `http://www.domain.com/` method to avoid confusion.

# Changing the Position of an Image

Have you ever been to a page that has a flying banner? There are many uses for this catchy display option. Some take this to an extreme, but for now, we'll keep it simple. This is a great exercise to quickly understand dynamic positioning concepts.

We'll use both absolute and relative positioning techniques. The first position is absolute, and the second position is relative to the first absolute position. You can use an increment operator (++) to change the document coordinates by ones if you wish, or even jump in increments of ten (or any given number, really) with the addition operator (+). The style.left attribute is used to give the image position in pixels. You can state a static value here, or you can use a variable or array item to arrive at the new coordinate through scripted action.

The image can be any dimension or format, as long as the format is supported by the browser. Changing the image dynamically is also a good effect.

We use the getElementById() method to access the display properties for that image. This includes its position on the page. The id attribute must be stated with the IMG element to allow the browser to figure out what element is to be positioned.

*Listing 6-25.* Working with image positioning

```
<html>
<head>
<script type="text/javascript">
function moveleft() {
      document.getElementById('image').style.position="absolute";
      document.getElementById('image').style.left="0";
}
function moveback() {
      document.getElementById('image').style.position="relative";
}
</script>
</head>
<body>
<img id="image" src="imageon.gif" onmouseover="moveleft()"
onmouseout="moveback()">
</body>
</html>
```

To change back to the original position, a relative positioning method is used. It calls the original location of the image on the page and acts accordingly. If you're going to move an image within a table in the page, you must account for the area that the image will be moved within or the table will automatically alter to fit the new image position. For example, if you were to move a 100-pixel-wide image 10 pixels in both directions, you would have to have a space given in the TD element containing it to be 120 pixels wide – 10 pixels to the left, 10 pixels to the right, and the original 100-pixel-wide image.

# Changing the Background Image

You can change the background image of the entire document simply by changing that parameter of the BODY tag. We'll use the document.body.background statement to accomplish this. The background image may be any format supported by the browser. Its location may be stated as absolute or relative.

According to normal functionality, the background image to be displayed will be displayed in its actual dimensions. If the image is larger than the browser window area, the portions of the image that are larger than the window will not be displayed. If the background image is smaller than the browser window, the image will be repeated (tiled) to fill the remaining background area.

***Listing 6-26.*** Changing the background image

```
<html>
<head>
<script type="text/javascript">
function bgChange(bg) {
      document.body.background=bg;
}
</script>
</head>
<body>
<table width="300" height="100">
<tr>
      <td onmouseover="bgChange('image1.jpg')" background="image.jpg"></td>
      <td onmouseover="bgChange('image2.jpg')" background="image2.jpg"></td>
      <td onmouseover="bgChange('image3.jpg')" background="image3.jpg"></td>
</tr>
</table>
</body>
</html>
```

Also note that this can be used within a table – not just the entire displayed document. Just change the DOM statement given in the JavaScript function in the head of the document. A table has the option of displaying an image as the background, so it might be a good idea to look into this. Use the getElementById.style.background statement in this case. Give the location of the image as needed and apply with an onLoad event handler to display the background image when the page is loaded or an onMouseOver event to display the background image when the user selects that.

# An Image Viewer

This is a great experiment to play with. You can use this basic application to achieve some startling results without using a server-side script. We use a preloader to download the image data into an array. We then reference the array items and display accordingly.

The getElementById() method is used to access the properties of each image. The images are then displayed. This can be taken a little further – such as putting together a slideshow or simply displaying the images in the way you have in mind.

***Listing 6-27.*** An in-browser image viewer

```
<html>
<head>
<script type="text/javascript">
myImages=new Array();
myImages[0]="image1.gif";
myImages[1]="bulbon.gif";
myImages[2]="landscape.jpg";
myImages[3]="image2.gif";
myImages[4]="bulboff.gif";
myImages[5]="smiley.gif";
imagecounter=myImages.length-1;
i=0;
function first() {
      document.getElementById('imageviewer').src=myImages[0];
      i=0;
}
function previous() {
     if (i>0) {
          i--;
          document.getElementById('imageviewer').src=myImages[i];
     }
}
function next() {
     if (i<imagecounter) {
          i++;
```

```
            document.getElementById('imageviewer').src=myImages[i];
        }
    }
function last() {
        document.getElementById('imageviewer').src=myImages[imagecounter];
        i=imagecounter;
    }
</script>
</head>
<body>
<center>
<form>
<input type="button" value="First" onclick="first()">
<input type="button" value="Previous" onclick="previous()">
<input type="button" value="Next" onclick="next()">
<input type="button" value="Last" onclick="last()">
</form>
<img id="imageviewer" src="image1.gif" width="100" height="30">
</center>
</body>
</html>
```

A single click accesses the next, previous, first, or last image given in the array stated in the JavaScript function in the head of the document. Four functions were created, each with a specific action to access an index item in the array. The original image doesn't have to even be seen – it can be a transparent image 1 pixel by 1 pixel in size or an image that is the same size and color as the page background.

# A Digital Clock

Clocks are everywhere, and so they should be in your web page. You can make them as prominent or discreet as your taste allows. In this example, we're displaying ten images as the digits of the clock. Each digit is a unique image that is preloaded into an array. We then display the images in increments of a second, minute, or hour.

***Listing 6-28.*** A simple digital clock

```
<html>
<head>
<script type="text/javascript">
function getDigits() {
num=new Array("0.gif","1.gif","2.gif","3.gif","4.gif","5.gif","6.gif","7.
gif","8.gif","9.gif");
time=new Date();
hour=time.getHours()
if (hour<10) {
     document.getElementById('hour1').src=num[0];
     h2="'" + hour + "'";
     h2=h2.charAt(1);
     document.getElementById('hour2').src=num[h2];
} else {
     h1="'" + hour + "'";
     h1=h1.charAt(1);
     document.getElementById('hour1').src=num[h1];
     h2="'" + hour + "'";
     h2=h2.charAt(2);
     document.getElementById('hour2').src=num[h2];
}
minute=time.getMinutes();
if (minute<10) {
     document.getElementById('minute1').src=num[0];
     m2="'" + minute + "'";
     m2=m2.charAt(1);
     document.getElementById('minute2').src=num[m2];
} else {
     m1="'" + minute + "'";
     m1=m1.charAt(1);
     document.getElementById('minute1').src=num[m1];
     m2="'" + minute + "'";
     m2=m2.charAt(2);
     document.getElementById('minute2').src=num[m2];
```

```
}
second=time.getSeconds();
if (second<10) {
        document.getElementById('second1').src=num[0];
        s2="'" + second + "'";
        s2=s2.charAt(1);
        document.getElementById('second2').src=num[s2];
} else {
        s1="'" + second + "'";
        s1=s1.charAt(1);
        document.getElementById('second1').src=num[s1];
        s2="'" + second + "'";
        s2=s2.charAt(2);
        document.getElementById('second2').src=num[s2];
}
}
function showTime() {
        timer=setTimeout("getDigits()",10);
        interval=setInterval("getDigits()",1000);
}
function stopInterval() {
        clearTimeout(timer);
        clearInterval(interval);
}
</script>
</head>
<body onload="showTime()" onunload="stopInterval()" bgcolor="#000000">
<img id="hour1" />
<img id="hour2" />
<img id="minute1" />
<img id="minute2" />
<img id="second1" />
<img id="second2" />
</body>
</html>
```

It looks a little more complicated than it actually is. The images are placed in an array. The date is read using the getSeconds(), getMinutes(), and getHours() methods. We then simply increment those values according to the seconds, minutes, and hours we state in increments of milliseconds. For each increment in milliseconds, the appropriate image is displayed from the array we preloaded.

# A Drop-Down Menu

This simple drop-down menu uses CSS rules and the hidden and visible attributes of the style object. The menu is always there – it's just set to hidden. When you mouse over it, the property is changed to visible and you see the menu. Simple.

We use the getElementById() method to access the page properties and change only the hidden or visible property. Use a menu as simple or as complicated as needed. It doesn't really matter. Change its appearance through the use of simple CSS rules. I've included eight rules, and there are many more than that.

*Listing 6-29.*  A drop-down menu system

```
<html>
<head>
<style>
body{font-family:arial;}
table{font-size:80%;background:black}
a{color:black;text-decoration:none;font:bold}
a:hover{color:#606060}
td.menu{background:lightblue}
table.menu {
    font-size:100%;
    position:absolute;
    visibility:hidden;
}
</style>
<script type="text/javascript">
function showmenu(elmnt) {
    document.getElementById(elmnt).style.visibility="visible";
}
```

```
function hidemenu(elmnt) {
    document.getElementById(elmnt).style.visibility="hidden";
}
</script>
</head>
<body>
<table width="100%">
<tr bgcolor="#FF8080">
    <td onmouseover="showmenu('tutorials')" onmouseout="hidemenu
    ('tutorials')">
        <a href="page15">Tutorials</a><br />
    <table class="menu" id="tutorials" width="120">
    <tr>
        <td class="menu"><a href="page1.html">List Item</a></td>
    </tr><tr>
        <td class="menu"><a href="page2.html ">List Item</a></td>
    </tr><tr>
        <td class="menu"><a href="page3.html ">List Item</a></td>
    </tr><tr>
        <td class="menu"><a href="page4.html ">List Item</a></td>
    </tr>
    </table>
    </td>
    <td onmouseover="showmenu('scripting')" onmouseout="hidemenu
    ('scripting')">
        <a href="page16.html ">Scripting</a
    <table class="menu" id="scripting" width="120">
    <tr>
        <td class="menu"><a href="page5.html ">List Item</a></td>
    </tr><tr>
        <td class="menu"><a href="page6.html ">List Item</a></td>
    </tr><tr>
        <td class="menu"><a href="page7.html ">List Item</a></td>
    </tr><tr>
        <td class="menu"><a href="page8.html ">List Item</a></td>
```

```
        </tr><tr>
                <td class="menu"><a href="page9.html ">List Item</a></td>
        </tr>
        </table>
        </td>
        <td onmouseover="showmenu('validation')" onmouseout="hidemenu
        ('validation')">
                <a href="page17.html">Validation</a>
        <table class="menu" id="validation" width="120">
        <tr>
                <td class="menu"><a href="page10.html "> List Item</a></td>
        </tr><tr>
                <td class="menu"><a href="page11.html "> List Item</a></td>
        </tr><tr>
                <td class="menu"><a href="page12.html "> List Item</a></td>
        </tr><tr>
                <td class="menu"><a href="page13.html "> List Item</a></td>
        </tr><tr>
                <td class="menu"><a href="page14.html "> List Item</a></td>
        </tr>
        </table>
        </td>
</tr>
</table>
</body>
</html>
```

The list items are displayed as they appear within the table given. Notice that there are a few nested tables used. You can do this in any complexity you need and include any valid HTML coding using any formatting options. You can even put images and/or a form with many input elements in each drop-down list.

# Create Inset or Outset Border Buttons

So when you've learned to use bulleted lists, you were introduced to the concept of inset and outset placed buttons. Each bulleted item is placed in relation to the beginning location of the UL or OL element. Each list item is then stated with an LI element. Inset bullets are set to the right of the starting location specified by the OL or UL element. Outset bullets are further to the left.

The style.borderStyle attribute works the same way. You are able to position the border in an inset or outset styled display. The easiest way to understand this is to simply run the script given in Listing 6-30.

***Listing 6-30.*** Creating inset or outset buttons

```html
<html>
<head>
<script type="text/javascript">
function inset(elmnt) {
     elmnt.style.borderStyle="inset";
}
function outset(elmnt) {
     elmnt.style.borderStyle="outset";
}
</script>
<style>
td {
     background:C0C0C0;
     border:2px outset;
}
</style>
</head>
<body>
<table width="80">
<tr>
     <td onmouseover="inset(this)" onmouseout="outset(this)">Item One</td>
</tr><tr>
     <td onmouseover="inset(this)" onmouseout="outset(this)">Item Two</td>
```

```
</tr><tr>
     <td onmouseover="inset(this)" onmouseout="outset(this)">Item Three</td>
</tr><tr>
     <td onmouseover="inset(this)" onmouseout="outset(this)">Item Four</td>
</tr>
</table>
</body>
</html>
```

We used the onMouseOver and onMouseOut to trigger the different border styles. You don't have to go back to the original style, however, and can adjust the bordering styles as needed. A good example of this is to create a display of the sections of a document the user has read or reviewed. When they're finished reviewing the entire document, all of the border styles will be the same, letting them know in an easy way that they're finished what they started.

It is an unusual occurrence that this code snippet is not supported in Microsoft Edge. The days of massive differences between the implementations of any given markups are over, for the most part. You can attribute this to increased public input and a very well-run and organized W3C.org (World Wide Web Consortium).

# A Description Menu

This is a good way to add some surprising functionality to your links. You can link to anything in a different document or to a place within the current document as provided by the attributes you use within the anchor tag. Links may be relative or absolutely stated. CSS rules that apply to a normal link apply and are given in the head of the document.

We use the getElementById() method to access the properties of the anchor element, in this case, to assign the locations and other attributes of the links.

***Listing 6-31.*** A descriptive menu feature

```
<html>
<head>
<style>
Table {
```

```
        background:black;
}
a {
        text-decoration:none;
        color:#000000;
}
th {
        width:150px;
        background:#FF8080;
}
td {
        font:bold;
        background:#ADD8E6;
}
</style>
<script type="text/javascript">
function get(txt) {
        document.getElementById('tip').innerHTML="txt";
}
function reset() {
        document.getElementById('tip').innerHTML=" ";
}
</script>
</head>
<body>
<table width="400">
<tr>
        <td><a href="page.html" onmouseover="get('Description')"
        onmouseout="reset()">Item One</a></td>
        <td rowspan="3" id="tip"></td>
</tr><tr>
        <td>
<a href="page1.html" onmouseover="get('Description')"
onmouseout="reset()">Item Two</a></td>
</tr><tr>
```

```
    <td><a href="page2.html" onmouseover="get('Description)"
    onmouseout="reset()">Item Three</a></td>
</tr>
</table>
</body>
</html>
```

I've put the links in a table, but they don't have to be. You can place them anywhere you like using any method you like, as long as they're able to be rendered by the browser.

# Create a Description Box for an Image

This series of instructions shows a small pop-up description according to whatever you're interested in showing. You place the descriptive text within the functions as they're placed in the document. The functions are triggered with an onMouseOver event handler and reset by calling a reset() method with an onMouseOut event handler.

Assign any CSS rules you like, as long as they're applicable to a textual link. If you'd like to play around, you can include many different formatting styles and any valid CSS rule that is reflected within the DOM specifications. There are many, some 400 of them.

***Listing 6-32.*** A description box for an image

```
<html>
<head>
<style>
table {
    background:black;
}
a {
    text-decoration:none;
    color:#000000;
}
td {
    font:bold;
    background:#ADD8E6;
}
```

```
</style>
<script type="text/javascript">
function get(image) {
    document.getElementById('tip').innerHTML="<img src='" + image + "' />";
}
function reset() {
    document.getElementById('tip').innerHTML=" ";
}
</script>
</head>
<body>
<table width="100%">
<tr>
    <td><a href="page1.html" onmouseover="get('image1.gif')"
    onmouseout="reset()">Item One</a></td>
</tr><tr>
    <td><a href="page2.html" onmouseover="get('image2.gif')"
    onmouseout="reset()">Item Two</a></td>
</tr><tr>
    <td><a href="page3.html" onmouseover="get('image3.gif')"
    onmouseout="reset()">Item Three</a></td>
</tr>
</table>
</body>
</html>
```

I have placed the links inside a table and have provided a reset() method to clear the descriptive text from being displayed. You might not want to do this, though – just leave the descriptions up if you need to, without calling a reset() method.

# A Sliding Horizontal Menu

These menus have always been very popular because they're very impressive and useful. We use a series of CSS rules to assign formatting and positioning. The JavaScript functions are called with an onMouseOver event handler to open the menu and an onMouseOut event handler to close the menu.

The getElementById() method is used to access the display properties for the initial formatting and display options. We then alter these options according to the directions given in the rest of the script.

The speed that the menu opens with is an option that can be set according to your preference. If you'd like a quicker slide, decrease this value. If you'd like a slower slide, increase the value.

**Listing 6-33.** A sliding horizontal menu

```html
<html>
<head>
<style>
body {
     font-family:arial;
}
a {
     color:black;text-decoration:none;font:bold;
}
a:hover {
     color:#606060;
}
td.menu {
     background:lightblue;
}
table.nav {
     background:black;
     position:relative;
     font: bold 80% arial;
     top:0px;
     left:-135px;
}
</style>
<script type="text/javascript">
var i=-135;
var intHide;
var speed=3;
```

```
function showmenu() {
      clearInterval(intHide);
      intShow=setInterval("show()",10);
}
function hidemenu() {
      clearInterval(intShow);
      intHide=setInterval("hide()",10);
}
function show() {
      if (i<-12) {
            i=i+speed;
            document.getElementById('myMenu').style.left=i;
      }
}
function hide() {
      if (i>-135) {
            i=i-speed;
            document.getElementById('myMenu').style.left=i;
      }
}
</script>
</head>
<body>
<table id="myMenu" class="nav" width="150" onmouseover="showmenu()"
onmouseout="hidemenu()">
<tr>
      <td class="menu"><a href="page1.html">Item One</a></td>
</tr><tr>
      <td class="menu"><a href="page2.html ">Item Two</a></td>
</tr><tr>
      <td class="menu"><a href="page3.html">Item Three</a></td>
</tr><tr>
      <td class="menu"><a href="page4.html">Item Four</a></td>
</tr><tr>
      <td class="menu"><a href="page5.html">Item Five</a></td>
```

```
</tr>
</table>
</body>
</html>
```

You may include any valid HTML coding into your sliding menu. A few examples of this are forms, images, and embedded files for video and audio. By segregating the class= attributes, you're able to assign specific formatting to every element within your menu on an individual basis.

# A Click-Driven Horizontal Sliding Menu

So you've all seen the horizontal menus that zoom out when you mouse over them, but it is entirely possible to change this if you find that it just isn't what you're looking for. You can initiate the menu with a click of the mouse (an onClick event handler) and slide it back with an onMouseOut event that collapses the menu. If you'd like to have the menu slide out when the button goes down and slide back when it goes up, use the onMouseDown and onMouseUp event handlers.

Any CSS rule can be applied, and any HTML element can be used within the menu. You can even put a form on it if you so choose. Definitely add some images, small or large, to add some appeal.

We use the getElementById() method to access the properties of the page elements and act upon them. A single onClick event handler executes the JavaScript functions within the head of the document, and the menu slides out.

*Listing 6-34.* A click-driven horizontal menu

```
<html>
<head>
<style>
body{
      font-family:arial;
}
a {
      color:black;text-decoration:none;font:bold;
}
```

```
a:hover {
     color:#606060;
}
td.menu {
     background:lightblue;
}
table.nav {
     background:black;
     position:relative;
     font: bold 80% arial;
     top:0px;
     left:-135px;
     margin-left:3px;
}
</style>
<script type="text/javascript">
var i=-135;
var c=0;
var intHide;
var speed=3;
function show_hide_menu() {
     if (c==0)
     {
          c=1;
          clearInterval(intHide);
          intShow=setInterval("show()",10);
     } else {
          c=0;
          clearInterval(intShow);
          intHide=setInterval("hide()",10);
     }
}
function show() {
     if (i<-12)
     {
```

```
            i=i+speed;
            document.getElementById('myMenu').style.left=i;
        }
    }
function hide() {
        if (i>-135)
        {
            i=i-speed;
            document.getElementById('myMenu').style.left=i;
        }
    }
</script>
</head>
<body>
<table id="myMenu" class="nav" width="150" onclick="show_hide_menu()">
<tr>
        <td class="menu"><a href="page1.html">Item One</a></td>
</tr><tr>
        <td class="menu"><a href="page2.html">Item Two</a></td>
</tr><tr>
        <td class="menu"><a href="page3.html">Item Three</a></td>
</tr><tr>
        <td class="menu"><a href="page4.html">Item Four</a></td>
</tr><tr>
        <td class="menu"><a href="page5.html">Item Five</a></td>
</tr>
</table>
</body>
</html>
```

There can be as many menu items as you wish, and they don't have to be in one single column as I have them here. Multicolumn menus are entirely possible – if it can be rendered in a normal page, you can include it in your menu.

# Return the Cursor's Coordinates

If you're going to be using any type of positioning in your web development, it will be absolutely necessary to know and understand how coordinates are recalculated, returned, and altered by the browser. Coordinates in a browser are represented by the X axis and Y axis. Each has their own objects and methods to read or alter the X and Y values built in to the browser.

We'll use the event.clientX and event.clientY attributes to return the values of the current position of the exact tip of the mouse pointer as it sits on the web page the moment the function is triggered. The value is returned very quickly, and you can act on and alter that value through scripted action just as quickly.

You'll see this code in every page you've seen that has movable buttons or flying banners. It's a universal operation, so it's best to take a long look at it and commit it to memory. It's much simpler than it sounds.

***Listing 6-35.*** Returning the cursor's coordinates

```
<html>
<head>
<script type="text/javascript">
function show_coords(event) {
      x=event.clientX;
      y=event.clientY;
      alert("X coords: " + x + ", Y coords: " + y);
}
</script>
</head>
<body onclick="show_coords(event)">
Click Anywhere To Return The Mouse Position
</body>
</html>
```

Notice how easy this is? It is very important, though. The script is set up to show an alert box when you click anywhere on the document, as shown through the use of the onClick event handler that has been placed as an attribute of the BODY element.

# Make Your Text Follow the Cursor

You can instruct the browser to have a string of text follow the cursor around anywhere in the active window. We first determine the X and Y coordinates of the mouse pointer. Then we determine some idea as to what the text should look like and assign them with common CSS rules. Positioning is determined and the text is set to follow the pointer, while the X and Y coordinates are being generated and passed along the bubbling order of the JavaScript functions in the head of the document.

The text is actually always there – we just set it to hidden with the style.visibility attribute and to visible when we need to. The onMouseMove event handler triggers the JavaScript functions when you move the cursor on the X or Y axis 1 pixel. If you stay still, so will the text.

To have a finer degree of control over the rendering of the moving – if it looks jerky – just alter the amount that the X or Y axis is incremented with every iteration of the script. A smaller value will result in a smoother look but might lag a little behind if you're showing a lot of text trailing behind the cursor or if the computer is being used heavily. If this is a concern, increase the increment of the positioning and the text will move quicker and will stay with the cursor.

***Listing 6-36.*** Making the text follow the pointer

```
<html>
<head>
<script type="text/javascript">
function cursor(event) {
    document.getElementById('trail').style.visibility="visible";
    document.getElementById('trail').style.position="absolute";
    document.getElementById('trail').style.left=event.clientX+10;
    document.getElementById('trail').style.top=event.clientY;
}
</script>
</head>
<body onmousemove="cursor(event)">
<span id="trail" style="visibility:hidden">Cursor Text</span>
</body>
</html>
```

You can assign an image to follow the cursor as well. Just state a simple IMG element with the same given preceding attributes for the textual version. The coordinate system works the same for text as it does for images, as it's initially based not on the location of the text or image, but on the position of the mouse pointer.

## Summary

We covered a lot of ground in this chapter. We explored how HTML, CSS, DOM, and JavaScript work together in a web page. We touched on formatting and design. We introduced concepts such as creating and loading variables and arrays – and using what is contained within them.

# CHAPTER 7

# Installing and Using the Perl Server

This chapter is brief, as there is only so much you need to know to install and use a Perl server. For the most part, most operations are simple and intuitively obvious.

## Where's Perl?

As mentioned in a previous chapter, the first line of any Perl script is called the *shebang*. It is the location on the hard drive of the Perl executables. On Linux operating systems, it's usually #!/usr/bin/perl.

On the Windows operating system, the location of Perl is a little convoluted and not very intuitive. All of the Perl .msi packages available install directly to c:\Program Files\ Perl\bin\perl.exe. This has the very irritating drawback of the space between the word Program and the word Files throwing errors because scripts and other programs get stuck by that pesky space. To counter that, the path to Perl should be #!c:/progra~1/perl/ bin/perl.exe.

I recommend installing Perl to the root of the C drive, as follows: C:\Perl\bin\perl. exe. You would have to specify this during the installation of the Perl binaries.

## Preparing Your Workstation

As with most software installations, you will have to close all programs, being sure to save your work first. Once all programs are shut down and your work is saved, double-click the .msi package you downloaded to begin the installation. The name of this .msi package depends on the flavor of Perl you decided to use.

123

© Thomas Valentine 2023
T. Valentine, *Database-Driven Web Development*, https://doi.org/10.1007/978-1-4842-9792-6_7

# Installing the Perl Server

Once you click the .msi package, the installation will be halted by a window that asks for permission for the installing program to make changes to your operating system and install the program. If you decline, the installation promptly halts.

There will invariably be a logo screen as the first window of the install program. Some flavors of Perl put the End User License Agreement in the first window. If the agreement isn't on the first window, it'll be on the second. Click "I Agree" to accept the terms of the contract.

Next up is a window that either asks what to install or where to install it to on your hard drive. This location, by default, is C:\Program Files\Perl for a Windows workstation and #!/usr/bin/perl for a Linux workstation.

If the second window wasn't the installation option, the third will be. I recommend you install everything. This includes the Perl executables and support libraries as well as the literature on the use of your Perl server. Including the literature increases the install time by about two minutes.

# Topics to Consider

One of the topics to consider during installation is simply the location of Perl. I recommend your path on a Windows operating system be C:\Perl. This goes against the default path, but you'll actually benefit from it further down the road.

Some programs don't like the space between Program and Files if you were to use the default path during installation. There is a workaround to this, which is a bit unintuitive. The path C:\Progra~@\Perl is the path that some programs that don't like the space will require to operate. Installing to C:\Perl allows these legacy programs to find Perl without adding extra work such as including PATH statements, which is a direct change to the operating system and is beyond the scope of this book.

# Perl Is Always Ready

One of the best things about Perl is you don't have to start a server or service to use the full capabilities of the Perl server. It is always ready to take on work. The first line of every Perl script gives the location to the Perl executables. The Perl server springs into action with minimal fuss.

Perl is an inline language, meaning that execution begins at the top of the script and moves down, following the instructions as they are placed within the body of the script.

# Installing Perl Modules

On a Perl server, extra functionality comes from Perl modules. A Perl module is a software package that enhances and extends the capabilities of your standard Perl installation.

The most oft-used Perl modules come standard with the installation binaries and can be identified by their .pm extension. Two Perl modules that we'll be using extensively are DBD.pm and DBI.pm. They allow interaction between the Perl script and the database server (that you'll install in the next chapter).

There are two methods of installing a Perl module – using CPAN.bat and PPM.bat. They both work fine most of the time, but since there are thousands of Perl modules to choose from, you might have to switch between CPAN and PPM in order to have a successful installation. That is, if one doesn't work, try the other.

There are some modules that rely on other modules to complete their functionality. The aforementioned DBD.pm has to be installed before DBI.pm is installed, for example. If you leave out DBD.pm and only install DBI.pm, you'll get fatal errors to be thrown. Most of the time, the installing program knows what modules need to be installed and installs them automatically, with minimum fuss.

# CPAN.bat

CPAN stands for Comprehensive Perl Archive Network. It is the means by which you'll be installing the Perl modules used in the projects in later chapters. The website for the Perl modules is CPAN.org. It is an easy-to-use and complete list of all of the functionality that Perl has to offer.

To start CPAN.bat, simply double-click the link that you'll find in the Perl/bin directory. A dialog box will open with a flashing cursor, signifying that CPAN.bat is ready to work. Then type a question mark at the command prompt, and the CPAN.bat help options will appear as shown in Figure 7-1.

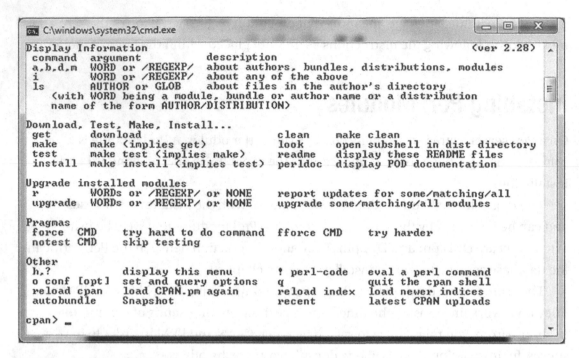

*Figure 7-1.* *CPAN.bat help options*

Simply type instructions such as "Install DBD" and CPAN.bat will chug and install the DBD.pm module. Do this before DBI.pm is installed, as stated earlier in this chapter. As mentioned before, CPAN.bat usually knows what libraries are required to install the full capabilities of each module.

# The Perl Package Manager (PPM)

The Perl Package Manager is the other means to install Perl modules. Some say it's easier to use, and this is probably the case, but there are restrictions on what PPM can do. For example, CPAN.bat knows what libraries to install for pretty much every module created to date. PPM doesn't have a comprehensive database, so sometimes PPM won't work.

As with CPAN.bat, simply double-click the ppm.bat windows batch file. A command dialog box will be displayed. Enter the word "help" at the command prompt and the screen in Figure 7-2 will appear.

```
C:\windows\system32\cmd.exe

PPM interactive shell (11.11_04) - type 'help' for available commands.
PPM> help
Commands:
    exit                - leave the program.
    help [command]      - prints this screen, or help on 'command'.
    install PACKAGES    - installs specified PACKAGES.
    quit                - leave the program.
    query [options]     - query information about installed packages.
    remove PACKAGES     - removes the specified PACKAGES from the system.
    search [options]    - search information about available packages.
    set [options]       - set/display current options.
    verify [options]    - verifies current install is up to date.
    version             - displays PPM version number

PPM>
```

**Figure 7-2.** *PPM.bat*

As you can see, PPM is easier to use than CPAN.bat due to its lack of optional commands. While most modules will install just fine, be ready for when one or two modules you require won't install with PPM.

# Commonly Used Perl Modules

As you'll see in a later chapter, there is a module for pretty much everything that is possible on the Internet to date. Also mentioned was the fact that some Perl modules require that supporting modules be installed first.

In the projects to come in later chapters, you'll see the list of Perl modules required for the Perl scripts to work stated at the top of every script. I've found that the most oft-used modules that aren't in the standard distribution are as follows:

- Size.pm

- Resize.pm

- File::Copy

- Image::Magick

They are all intuitively obvious as to what they do by their names. Size.pm is used to return the size, measured in pixels, of an image. Resize.pm is used to resize an image to a larger or smaller size. As with all things Perl, there are a couple of details to keep in mind. Both the size.pm and resize.pm modules will only work with jpg (jpeg), gif, and png file formats.

The Image::Magick module requires that its software package be installed on your server in order to be able to access the higher capabilities of the Image::Magick module. There are both source code (for Linux) and binaries (for Windows) available to be downloaded and installed. The installation is very easy and simple on both operating systems.

Image::Magick supports pretty much every image file format in creation. With it, you can manipulate images via scripted action, as touched on in Chapter 6.

# Summary

In this chapter, we installed Perl and reviewed the finer points of a typical Perl installation. We discussed Perl modules and how they work. We also explored installing Perl modules with CPAN.bat and PPM.bat.

# CHAPTER 8

# Installing and Using the MySQL Database Server

The MySQL database server has been around for years and as such is a robust and practical piece of software. Its features are many and are powerful. MySQL is the most oft-used database in the world. It has to be good to earn that designation. Quite the accomplishment. Even compared to giant database vendors like Oracle, MySQL stands up to the task. SQL (Structured Query Language) is a simple database language to learn, and the server is easy to install, use, and configure.

MySQL is a memory-resident piece of software, meaning that the entire functional pieces of the server are loaded into memory and are ready to execute queries without pausing to load more software into memory to accomplish the task at hand.

## Locating and Downloading the MySQL Server Binaries

The software you're looking for to install the MySQL server is available from MySQL. com. They offer the MySQL database for free.

The pay ware package is for production environments that require high-level functionality such as clustering and other technologies that are required to accommodate high-traffic networks. They sell you the software, and it comes with technical support options. Most believe it is a better piece of software than the free flavor, and in terms of capability, they're right. The binary package from MySQL.com is designed for websites and doesn't offer support for clustering or database farms.

© Thomas Valentine 2023
T. Valentine, *Database-Driven Web Development*, https://doi.org/10.1007/978-1-4842-9792-6_8

# What's a Beta?

If you've installed software in the past, you've probably run past an option to download a beta. Betas are software pieces that are in the process of being debugged. They are written but still contain errors or omissions. Expect errors from a beta.

It is not recommended that you use a beta for your active database server, as there is going to be errors that will cause headaches to ensue. They're fun to play around with, but running it live will just frustrate you.

# Preparing Your Workstation

It is recommended that you save all of your work and close down any active software before you start the installation process. Having software run that might interfere or be incompatible with the server is a real threat to the basic health of your installation as well as the workstation as a whole.

It is also recommended that you restart the workstation before you begin the installation. This will ensure you're working with an operating system that is not running with errors or shortcomings instituted by other software.

# Installing the MySQL Server

As with most software installations, the first thing you're asked is if you'll allow changes to be made to the operating system. Click Yes or No. Yes will allow the installation of the MySQL server to begin. No will promptly end the installation.

The first dialog box of the installation program to open is the setup type. There are five different installation options. While they all should be explored eventually, for purposes of discussion, we'll go with the Full setup type. This will install every feature and ability that is possible with the binary, including the official manuals.

The MySQL server installation and configuration typically take about ten minutes, depending on the resources that are available to you and what you've chosen to install. You'll be asked for basic things like usernames and passwords and networking concerns that we'll discuss as needed.

The MySQL install packages come in two general installation types: a small, 4- or 5-megabyte installer and a 450-megabyte installer. The difference between the two is in the way the installation is allowed to proceed. The small package is a web installer. If you use this package, the installation will start but will eventually pause to download the rest of the setup software. The big one is the entire installation package in one MSI installer.

It is recommended that you download the entire 450 megabyte package so you can still install and configure the workstation should Internet connectivity become a problem (Figure 8-1).

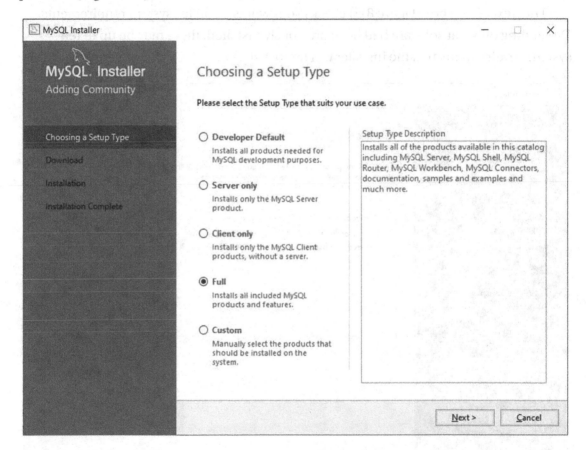

***Figure 8-1.***  *Choosing the setup type*

It is intuitively obvious as to what each installation type does. Select each option to cause a brief description of what will happen being given in the Setup Type Description box to the right of the radio buttons. The installer is a very stable and capable entity.

We selected Full because it is handy to have all manuals and documentation at your fingertips on the local workstation. The manuals and tools included with a Full installation are indispensable.

If you've installed the Full version, you'll have all of the capabilities ready to use. If you installed the Developer version, you won't get the literature or tools included in the Full installation, but your installation will still be very capable.

Selecting the Custom installation will give you the wide array of available features, selected through radio buttons, check boxes, and drop-down lists.

The next dialog box (Figure 8-2) checks your workstation for system requirements. Depending on what software had been previously installed, there may be up to ten system requirements that the installer will try to install.

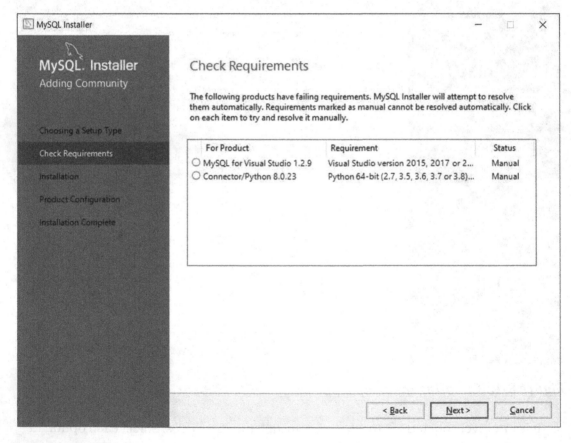

*Figure 8-2.* *Checking for system requirements*

There may be a few system requirements that the installer can't install. These requirements aren't normally needed unless you're using tools that don't pertain to serving data to web pages. As you can see in Figure 8-2, the only two system requirements that are left for full capability aren't normally used on Internet sites and are beyond the scope of this book.

The requirements that are labeled as "Manual" require you to locate, download, and install supporting software to end up with a full installation with full capabilities. Like I mentioned, these products aren't typically used in today's web pages.

As you can see in Figure 8-3, there are ten products ready to be installed. This is typical of a Full installation. You're able to do pretty much anything that is required of a modern web page with these products.

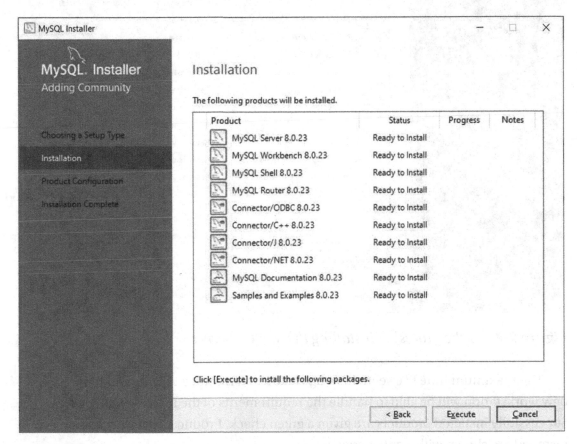

***Figure 8-3.*** *Software to be installed*

It should be noted that now is the time that the operating system will halt the installation should there not be enough free space on the hard drive you're installing to. The downloaded MSI is about 450 megabytes. Expect more space to be used after unpacking the compressed files, in the range of 520 megabytes. The total space required, then, is about a gigabyte. Be sure you have enough space on your hard drive. Examine Figure 8-4:

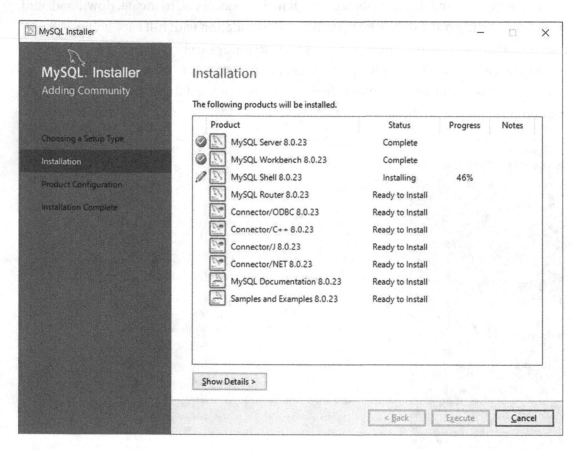

***Figure 8-4.***  *In the process of installing the MySQL server*

The maximum time I've seen this stage take is ten minutes. Any moderately new workstation will be able to handle the requirements of the installer with ease. Successfully installed products are given a green check. Products currently being installed are shown with a cute pencil icon.

This section is where you basically sit back and watch the installer do its thing. The installation will have reported errors by now, so it's a good bet that the installation is going to be successful. If you'd like to see exactly what is going on in real time, click the "Show Details" button.

There might be trouble with the installation if software that accesses the same resources that the installer does is running. Be sure to shut everything down that you can, especially software that uses the Internet or communications. Don't keep the web browser you used to download the binaries running either.

As you can see in Figure 8-5, all of the products were successfully installed. Now the installation program will present a series of dialog boxes that will ask for usernames and passwords. I recommend you write this down in many different locations until it becomes secondhand knowledge that you'll be using several times a day to configure your installation.

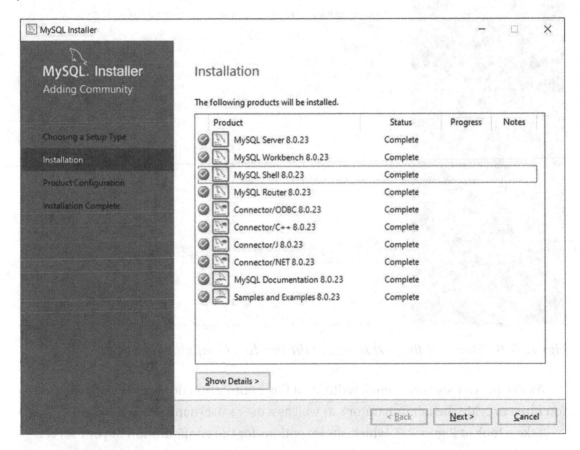

*Figure 8-5.* *All products completely installed*

Of particular note, the MySQL Documentation installed contains handy tips and tools for your everyday database administration duties. Do take a look and have a read. I've been using MySQL for two decades now, and I learn something new with every version of the MySQL Documentation and Samples and Examples.

Regardless of what type of installation you select, there are always going to be these three products (at least) that you'll have to provide some information for. The questions being asked are concerning root usernames and passwords as well as users' names and passwords (Figure 8-6).

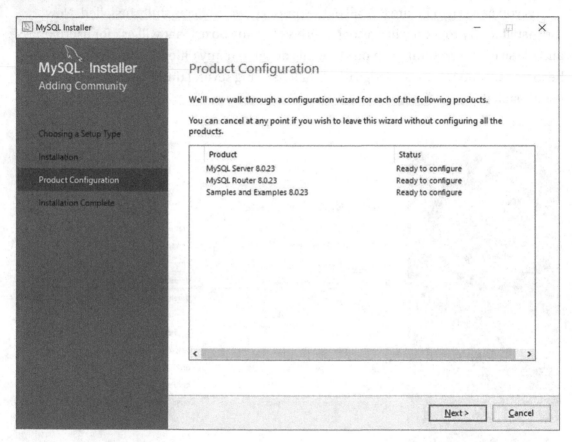

*Figure 8-6. Showing the first screen of the Product Configuration area*

As I've previously mentioned, write all of this information down in several locations. You must provide the administrator's as well as a user's username and password.

Take a look at Figure 8-7, which shows options for the configuration of your server on your local network. There are a few different Config Types to choose from. I suggest you keep your selection of Development Computer. This is because the other options assume that the workstation (now a server) is the main piece of software that is being run. The MySQL engine and supporting programs are loaded directly into memory. The rest of the available memory that hasn't been taken by the operating system is attached to the MySQL server.

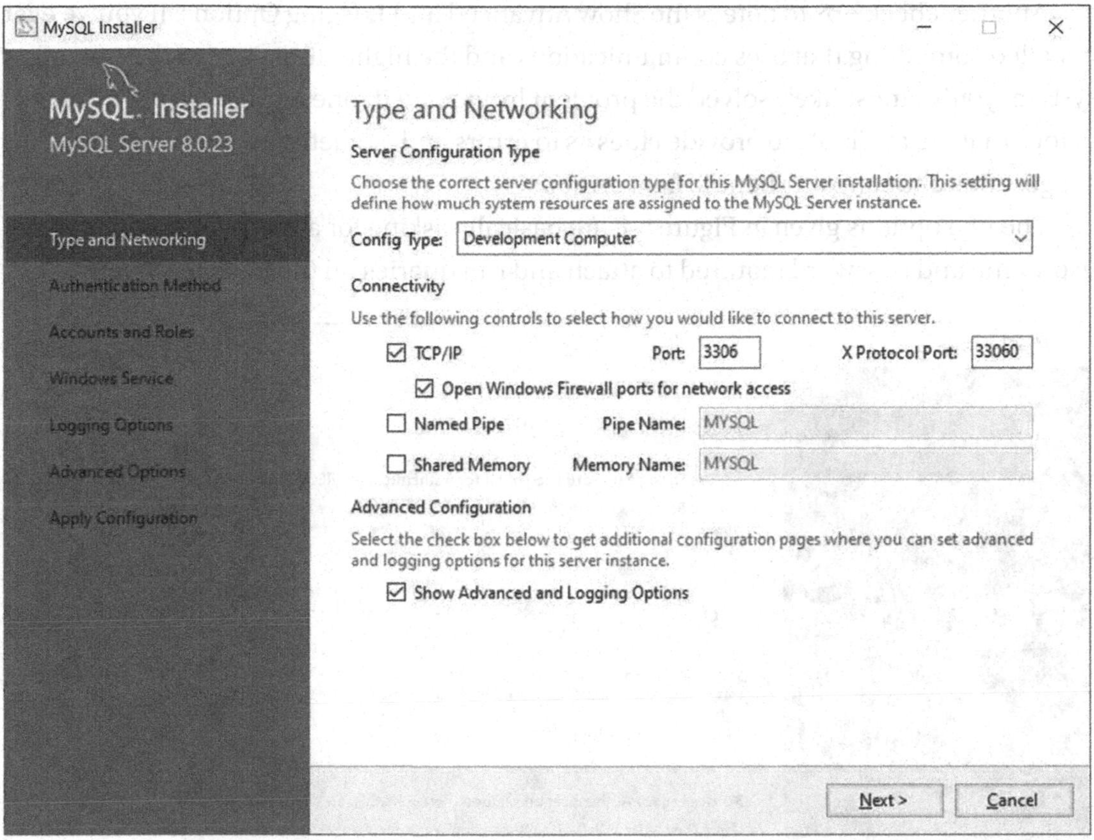

**Figure 8-7.**  *Setting network and installation options*

Figure 8-7 shows the options you have that are available via the MySQL installer. Always select TCP/IP. The default port, which is already filled in, should be written down with all of your usernames and passwords. Other technologies, such as the Apache web server, use mutually agreed-upon port numbers for each communications protocol. Every major server or tool gets its own port to connect on, which speeds things up, programmatically speaking.

There is also an option to use Windows Firewall to include some security for your future database use. TCP/IP is a very capable communications protocol that has been the primary protocol used on the Internet since the earliest days when the Internet was a research and development project.

Another check box to note is the Show Advanced and Logging Options. If you've ever installed something that uses communications and the higher functions of the operating system, you've most likely solved the problem by looking in one or many of the dozens of logs that are available to provide clues as to errors and, sometimes, to even give suggestions about how to handle fatal errors.

The two options given in Figure 8-8 are basically asking for a way to authenticate the username and password required to attach and run queries on the MySQL server.

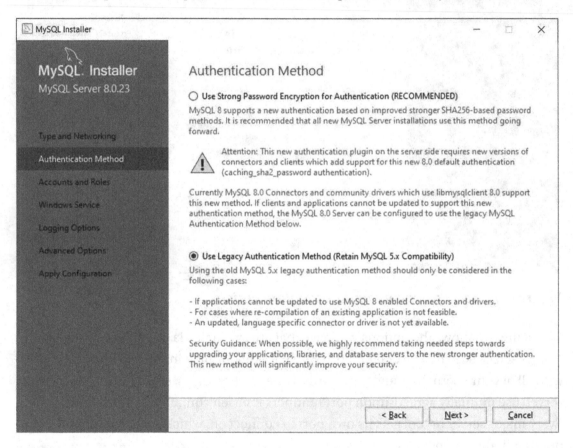

***Figure 8-8.*** *Two options for authentication method*

Because you're most likely not installing a dedicated database server, it is recommended that you select "Use Legacy Authentication Method." This is for backward compatibility with previous, out-of-date (but still used) servers. The last time the authentication method was changed or added to was when the MySQL server was in version 5.X.

You must specify a root username and password. Again, write this down in several locations until you've used it so much it becomes a second nature recollection when asked for authentication (Figure 8-9).

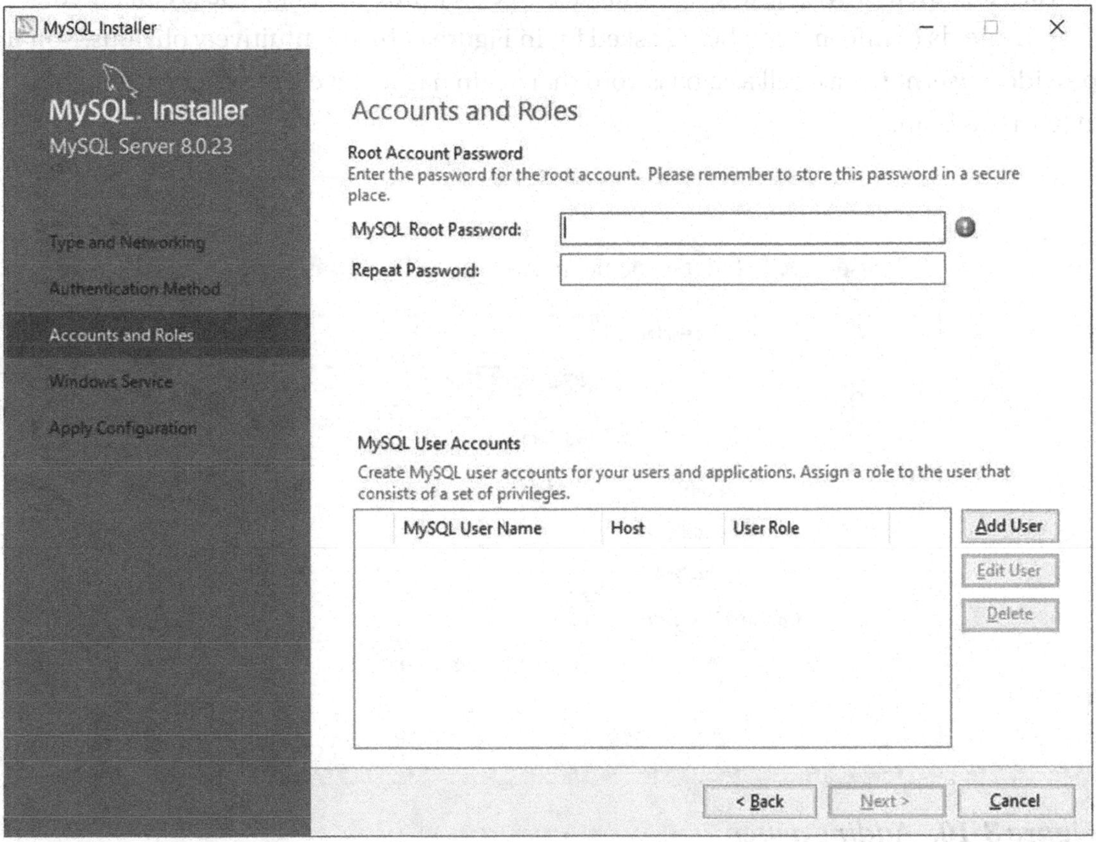

*Figure 8-9.  Setting administrative usernames and passwords*

There is a meter that displays the strength of the password. Use upper- and lowercase letters, numbers, and punctuation. Using these four types of characters for your passwords will result in a strong password that you have to write down until you know it with a moment's thought.

If your password strength is deemed weak, the installation program will not allow you to proceed. The password strength must be at least medium before the installer will allow you to continue.

It is recommended you create at least one user within this dialog box and assign administrative privileges to that newly created user. Using a superuser instead of the root account allows the security concerns of both the MySQL server and the operating system to work together, providing a secure transaction every time the database is consulted.

The fields of information being asked for in Figure 8-10 are intuitively obvious. You'll provide a username as well as a password that again has to have a password strength of at least medium.

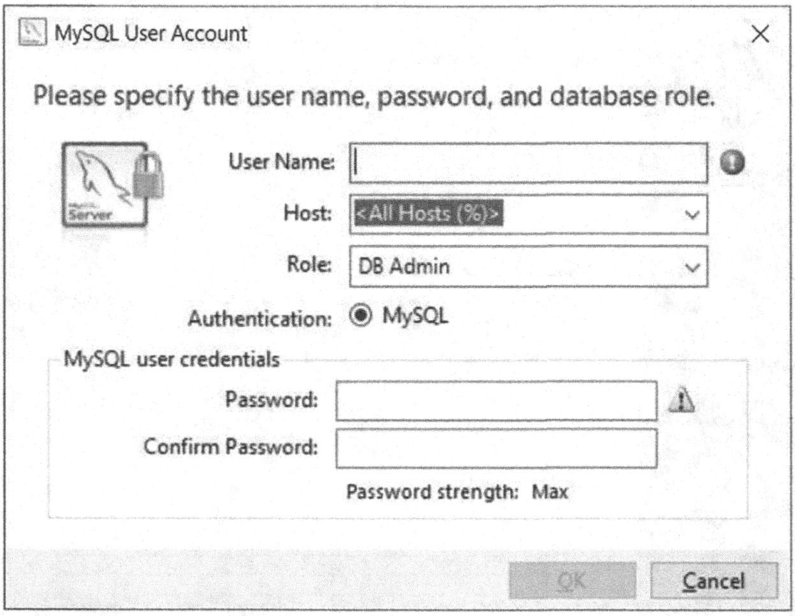

*Figure 8-10.  Adding a user*

Keep the role of DB Admin for this first user. Write down this username and password in several places. By now, you'll have about half a page of security information recorded that is essential to working with your MySQL server. Make several copies and give them to everyone that requires them.

Keep authentication to be resolved by MySQL. This is because the MySQL usernames and passwords are put through a more rigorous authentication protocol than do other entities such as the operating system.

When the password strength is medium or max, the OK button will become active, allowing you to proceed with the configuration of your server.

Figure 8-11 shows the option to configure the installation as a Windows Service. We don't want that, so take the check mark out of this field. You'll also see a check box to empty which tells the server to run at startup. You don't want this to happen, so make sure it is not checked.

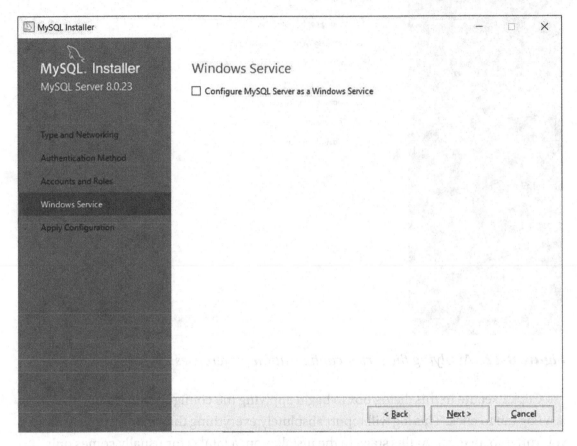

***Figure 8-11.*** *Selecting the configuration scheme*

If you were to run the MySQL server at startup, the rest of the operating system's capabilities will suffer and be narrower than if you started the MySQL server in console, which will be discussed in a coming section of this chapter.

The next dialog box that is displayed is the "Apply Configuration" section (Figure 8-12). Like I mentioned in a previous section of this chapter, if there were going to be any errors thrown by the installation, they would have been thrown by now. It's a good bet that your installation configuration will be applied successfully.

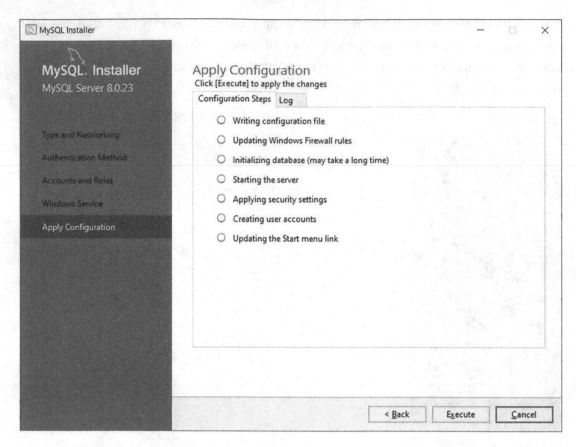

*Figure 8-12.* *Applying the server configuration preferences*

Click Execute in this dialog box to begin applying the configuration. Notice that there is a Log tab to click. This log will report absolutely everything that is being done should you run into an error. At this stage in the installation, a fatal error usually comes only from running out of disk space or processor utilization errors and incompatibilities.

This process takes a few minutes. You'll notice the pointer turn to hourglasses and working rings as the configuration progresses. If you've enabled a firewall, you'll either be asked to allow the MySQL server to provide authentication or bypass the firewall's authentication entirely. My advice is to have the firewall disregard MySQL queries, allowing them to pass beyond the firewall's area of influence.

This bypass is so you can practice using dedicated MySQL servers, perhaps in a multiple server setup. As you'll see in the chapters to come, MySQL teams well with Perl and the Apache web server. A common multiple server setup is to use three separate physical servers: one for the database server, one for the Perl scripting server, and one server as the file server.

## Start the MySQL Server

Starting the MySQL server via the command line is a simple task. This short command is all it takes to begin the startup : `mysql -u root -p`. Below the user is the root, server. After pressing Enter, you'll be asked for a username and password. Supply them from the page of usernames and passwords you have accrued and hopefully memorized already.

```
mysql -u root -p
```

# Summary

In this chapter, we discussed the installation and configuration of the MySQL database server. You learned how to turn your workstation into a powerful database server. In the chapters to come, the knowledge given in this chapter will be invaluable. Read on; there's quite a way to go before we're finished.

# CHAPTER 9

# Installing and Using the Apache Web Server

The Apache web server has as its core function the ability to serve web pages. It is a highly specialized and powerful software application that is being used to serve billions of web pages daily. The Apache web server is the single most oft-used web server on the Internet today.

Apache's most basic function is to serve static, unchanging HTML documents. This has the benefit of being the easiest method to implement – HTML is a simple language. If your site as you envision it is a simple affair, then by all means explore that. If you'd like dynamically created web pages that are driven by a powerful database, then read on. Apache can be used with Perl to generate web pages according to the rules given in a Perl script. This is more complicated than the static HTML method, but the extra thought, planning, and time are well worth the effort. The rewards for your hard work will be some very powerful and capable websites that will catch your user's attention and hold it.

Apache may work with several programming languages, be they scripted or compiled languages. Apache provides for a wide range of data-crunching abilities through the use of these various programming languages. It is a versatile and well-made product.

## Handling Errors

Apache has an error page for pretty much everything. As you'll see in the chapters to come, these error pages are indispensable when something goes wrong, usually in the configuration of Apache via the httpd.conf file. This configuration file will be explained in its entirety in the pages to come.

© Thomas Valentine 2023
T. Valentine, *Database-Driven Web Development*, https://doi.org/10.1007/978-1-4842-9792-6_9

Before starting the installation, it is recommended that you "ping the stack," which is a technical term for the readiness of the operating system to carry out whatever function you may be installing.

If the software and/or hardware that controls communications on a Windows workstation fails, the first thing you do is ping the loopback address, as shown in Figure 9-1.

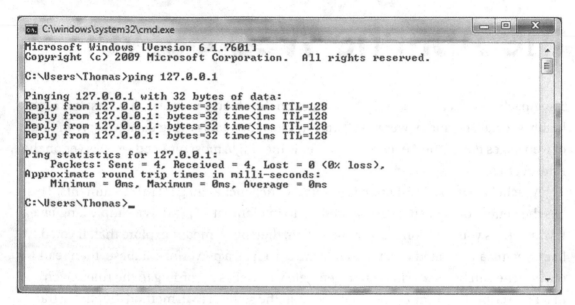

**Figure 9-1.**  *Pinging the local loopback address*

As you can see, there are four pings sent to 127.0.0.1 to ensure the operating system is functioning properly. If the operating system was in bad shape, you'd get an error message stating that the IP address was not found.

# Downloading and Installing the Apache Web Server Binaries

The first step in learning the Apache web server is to simply find the software. A simple Google search will tell you where to find Apache. Apache has been around for decades. The people that made it did and continue to do a very good job, and it's fairly easy to find the Apache binaries. This web server is developed with the Linux operating system in mind. It is ported to an executable package that the Windows operating system can deal with.

The binaries come in the form of an .msi package, which is the standard method of installing pretty much any software package on Windows. The installation is fairly basic. The learning curve sharpens when configuring the server and making it load on your Windows workstation.

# Allowing Changes to Your Operating System

The Windows operating system will first ask your permission to allow changes to your computer. The installation will halt if you decline this prompt. Every program that is installed on a Windows computer will start this way. The splash screen appears and is shown in Figure 9-2. Click Next to continue.

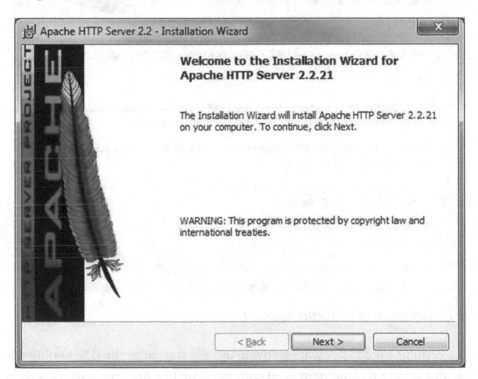

***Figure 9-2.*** *The splash screen of the Apache binary installation*

As with all software installations, a title page is displayed, showing important data like version and copyright statements.

Next comes the license agreement and legal stuff. You must review the information on this page to make sure you don't break your contract. It's pretty basic stuff.

The license agreement isn't all that lengthy or complicated. Most of it is basic rules and general use statements. Basically, you may use it as long as you don't alter the source code and expect it to work.

Another big statement in the agreement is that you will not sell the Apache server as your own product, even after altering the bulk of its source code.

Do have a read of the agreement. It only takes a few minutes but answers many questions about how you may and may not use this software.

Click the accept option as shown in Figure 9-3 and click Next.

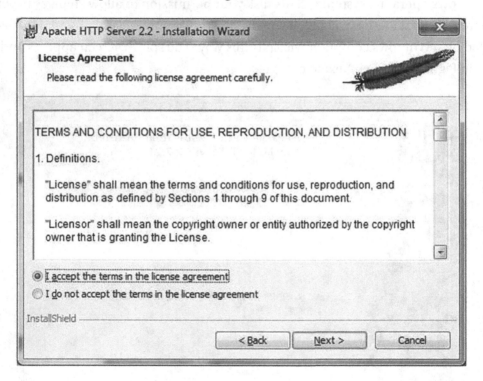

**Figure 9-3.**  *Accepting the license agreement*

The agreement used in freeware software usually started as the GNU Public License, which was the standard agreement used with freeware like Apache in its early days.

After the license agreement comes a window that you enter the local loopback address, 127.0.0.1, in two places, as shown in Figure 9-4. The page asks for a network domain Internet address, server name, administrator's email, and whether or not to install as a service or manually in console.

Here's where we have to explain things. A program – in this case, a server – can be run as a service of the operating system or as a program in console. A program run in console is run from the command line and displays its operating parameters in a black screen with white text.

The decision of which to use usually stems from what use you're going to be using the installation for. If Apache is installed on a server that will be running as a live web server serving pages over the Internet, install as a service. If it will be a web development workstation, select manual start, which will be in a command prompt. Starting in console still allows for the high functionality but won't be running constantly, such as when you aren't programming web pages.

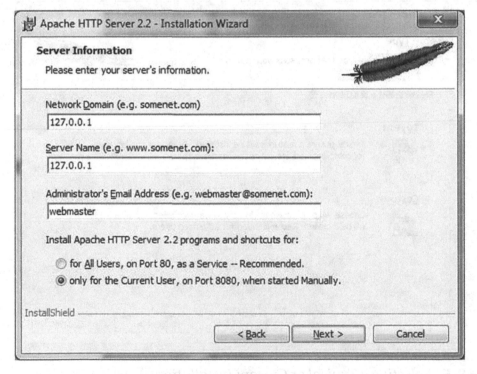

***Figure 9-4.*** *Filling out installation options*

You might be wondering why I use the local loopback address in both the Network Domain and Server Name fields. In order to serve a domain name, you would have to install and use a DNS (Domain Name Server). DNS servers match the IP address computers understand into a form that humans can understand, a domain name. While you can easily find a website with an IP address, for most people, remembering words instead of numbers works better should you want to find that site again. How the DNS server does all of this is beyond the scope of this book. In order to serve web pages for the workstation from the workstation, you need to use this address, which the operating system will automatically see as a local installation.

Installing Apache as a service requires administrative access. This is also required to stop and start the server, as you'll see if you install in this way.

Installing as a manually started program allows you to stop and start the Apache server simply and as needed, rather than it always being an active service that is taking up resources should you not be programming or serving pages. The next window, Figure 9-5, asks you to select a Custom or Typical installation. Select Custom and click Next.

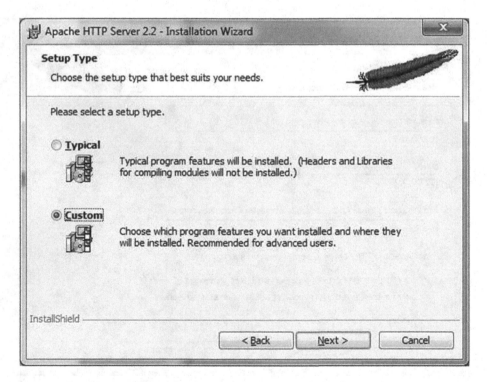

***Figure 9-5.***  *Selecting a Typical or Custom installation*

Ask for installation options. "Build Headers and Libraries" is not checked by default. Check it to install it. Set installation directory to be C:\Apache. You may have to change this field more than once. The installer wants you to name the Apache directory Apache2.2. There have been other places in this book that I've said to keep it as simple as possible. With a simple and easy-to-remember installation path, you don't have to look up directory or resource names. Do keep it simple. Examine Figure 9-6:

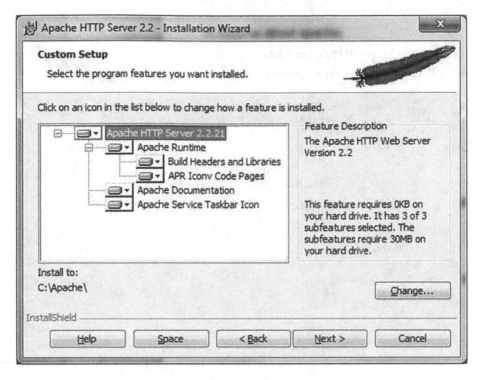

***Figure 9-6.*** *Specifying what is to be installed on the hard drive*

The next option is to click the Install button to begin the installation, as shown in Figure 9-7. You'll see a window with a progress bar that gives you an idea of the progress of your installation. The installation usually only takes a few minutes.

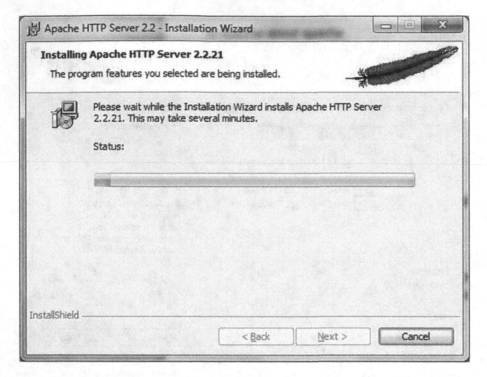

*Figure 9-7. The installation progress window*

After the progress bar disappears and your machine displays Figure 9-8, you've completed the installation. Now the Apache web server is on your workstation.

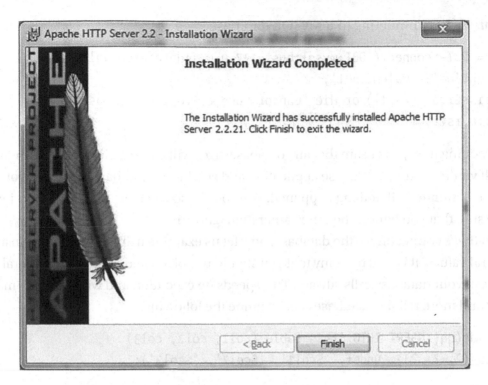

*Figure 9-8. Installation completed window*

# Apache and DBI.pm

The Perl DBI module is perhaps one of the best modules that have been put into production. With it, you are able to interact with a number of popular database servers in a timely and effective manner. The methods available from DBI make it a simple and effective affair to connect and interact with the database. All of the following examples assume you're using the current version of MySQL.

First, let us concentrate on connecting to the database. As with all things Perl, there are several distinct ways to do this, and all can be correct. We'll use what I've seen to be the most common syntax to connect to a MySQL database.

You're going to run into errors with databases for similar reasons that you do when using system calls. And just as you should always check the return code of your system calls, so should you always check the return status of your database calls. The easiest way to do this is by setting DBI's RaiseError attribute to 1. First, you would connect to the database and check the return. You would set the RaiseError attribute, as shown in Listing 9-1.

***Listing 9-1.*** Connecting to a MySQL database

```
$dbh = DBI->connect('DBI:mysql:host=127.0.0.1;database=tvalentine3',
'tvalentine', 'valentine1',
 {'RaiseError' => 1}) or die "Cannot Connect to the database:",
$DBI::errstr;
```

By doing this, you ensure that any database error will cause a die to be thrown by DBI. If you're writing a database application and you have a database error, you don't want to continue as if nothing happened. You could also catch the die in an eval – just make sure that you handle the error rather than ignore it.

So that's connecting to the database; now let us examine using placeholders instead of literal values. It is said by many that you should use placeholders instead of literal values in your database calls, always. This speeds up execution and will generally make a faster and more reliable database call. Examine the following:

```
$dbh->do(qq{INSERT INTO $this_table (col1, col2, col3)
VALUES (?, ?, ?)}, undef, '$col1', '$col2', '$col3');
```

We've inserted three columns in one row: col1, col2, and col3. What we've done is use placeholders as the values of the database insertion and provided variables with the actual data to be inserted. This is a simple and very fast method to perform a database call.

Now let us concentrate on SELECT statements. When you execute a SELECT statement, you would obviously want to get the data back as quickly as possible. The fastest way to do this is to use the bind_columns() and fetchrow_array() methods. bind_columns binds Perl variables to columns returned from your SELECT statement. For example, if you had the following SQL statement:

```
SELECT id, name, postid FROM $thistable
```

you'd want to bind three variables to the associated columns using the bind_columns() method. So you set up the variables, and then use bind_columns to bind them:

```
$sth->bind_columns(undef, \$id, \$name, \$postid);
```

The first argument to bind_columns is actually a hash reference specifying which DBI attributes to associate with this particular method. We don't want to associate any attributes with this particular method, so we'll just pass it undef, which is a completely OK thing to do. After you've called execute on your statement handle, you'll want to fetch the data. To do this, use the fetchrow_array() method, which fetches the next row and returns an array reference holding the field values. But you don't need to use that array reference, because you've got the column values bound to Perl variables, and you can just use those directly as shown in Listing 9-2.

***Listing 9-2.*** Selecting and retrieving three database items

```
while (@this_data = $sth->fetchrow_array()) {
    $id = $this_data[0];
    $name = $this_data[1];
    $postid = $this_data[2];
}
```

Each time you call fetchrow_array() on your statement handle, the values of the bound variables get updated.

Now let us take a look at mod_perl. Part of the purpose of mod_perl is to make Perl programs run much faster on the Apache web server. mod_perl accomplishes this by building a Perl interpreter into the web server and compiling your programs in memory. Thus, when it gets a new request, it maps that request onto a program compiled into memory, speeding things up considerably. If you're going to use DBI with mod_perl, you'll want to make sure that your database transactions are fast as well because you don't want the database being the bottleneck. The easiest way to accomplish this is to use the Apache::DBI module, which gives your programs persistent database connections. It does so by overriding the DBI connect method and keeping a cache of open database handles. One of the nicest things about Apache::DBI is that you won't have to modify your existing DBI code to use it. Just add the following before your "use DBI;" call:

```
use Apache::DBI;
```

You don't even have to take out the calls to disconnect, because Apache::DBI overrides those calls and makes sure that the handle doesn't actually get disconnected. This persistent connection speeds up execution by not having to connect to the database for each successive call to the script – an open database connection already exists.

# Starting the Apache Server

Starting your Apache server properly is a simple but important task. The first thing that httpd does when it is invoked is to locate and read the configuration file, httpd.conf. Within this file are the locations and settings for the Apache server's startup. You would specify what your root web location is, as well as dozens of other configuration directives.

During startup, the Apache server parses the httpd.conf file and applies the settings and directives you have within this file to that instance of the Apache server. The locations for your files can be anywhere on the current machine, either on a Linux operating system or a Windows operating system. It is understood that the user is adept on either or both of these operating systems before the installation of Apache.

When installing on a Windows operating system, you have the option of compiling the server's files from the source code or using a precompiled binary file. If you have a Windows version higher than Windows 98 and have the MSI installer up to date, you can download the .msi package to install Apache on your Windows machine. This is recommended, as it greatly simplifies the installation and ensures that any errors that may happen are handled and repaired by the installation program. The MSI installer is a program that has within it the rules for installing almost any program on the Windows operating system.

# Startup on a Windows Operating System

Startup on a Windows operating system is an easy affair. You simply state the path to the Apache.exe file along with a switch or two. You then give the location of the httpd.conf file and the root of the Apache source files' directory:

```
C:\Apache\bin\Apache.exe -w -f "C:\Apache\conf\httpd.conf" -d "C:\Apache"
```

First, we declared the path to the Apache.exe executable. We then included startup switches. Next, we included the path to the httpd.conf file for startup options. Finally, we gave the location of the root for the Apache installation.

# Stopping or Restarting the Server

In order to stop or restart Apache, you must send a signal to the running httpd processes. We'll examine stopping the server on a Windows machine first. This is as easy as pressing Ctrl+C in most cases, so we won't delve into stopping the Apache server on a

Windows machine very far. Instead, let us concentrate on the command-line switches that, save for the path to the executable, will be the same on a Linux as well as Windows operating system.

There are a number of switches that can be used to start or stop or restart the server. A full listing of these switches is beyond the scope of this book. However, the manual that comes with the Apache installation explains all of these switches and a great deal more – it is advised that you read the manual before using any of the higher functions inherent to Apache.

## Stopping the Apache Server

Stopping your Apache installation is a very easy affair, but it is one that must be covered in order for you to work with Apache in the future. The following command shows how to stop the Apache server on a Linux system:

```
apachectl -k stop
```

This example assumes you are within the working Apache directory. If you aren't, then you would use the entire path to the apachectl executable.

On Windows, there are two options for stopping the Apache web server that is started and is running in console. You can press Ctrl+C to exit or go to the Task Manager window and exit the program from there.

## Restarting the Apache Server, Gracefully

There are several ways to restart your server. You can use a command-line directive, or you can use the operating system to stop the Apache process. You would then have to restart according to the procedure given in an earlier section of this document. Examine the following command:

```
apachectl -k graceful
```

A graceful restart will restart the server after all waiting server calls have completed. The server then restarts and accepts new calls. This has the benefit of completing the waiting calls to the server before restarting. You would normally restart in this fashion after a configuration change within your httpd.conf file.

# Reviewing Runtime Configuration Directives

Runtime configuration directives are the commands and configuration notes that Apache uses to start the server. There are perhaps 200 of these directives, so a full explanation of these directives is beyond the scope of this book. See the manual that comes with the Apache distribution for an exhaustive and detailed explanation of every runtime configuration directive.

There are nine general types of runtime directives. They are server config, virtual host, directory, .htaccess, Core, MPM (Multi-Processing Modules), Base, Extension, and Experimental. Each of these runtime configuration types is an integral part of your Apache server's configuration and is read at server startup time.

The configuration directives are grouped into three basic sections within the httpd. conf file:

1. Directives that control the operation of the Apache server process as a whole (the "global environment").

2. Directives that define the parameters of the "main" or "default" server, which responds to requests that aren't handled by a virtual host. These directives also provide default values for the settings of all virtual hosts.

3. Settings for virtual hosts, which allow web requests to be sent to different IP addresses or hostnames and have them handled by the same Apache server process.

You'll get a feel for what each type of directive does with further use of the server and after reading the Apache manual.

## Setting the Server Root

The server root is the place where the Apache executable and configuration files are stored on the local machine.

```
ServerRoot "C:/Apache "
```

The ServerRoot directive tells the Apache server where the website documents, executables, and configuration files start.

# Setting the Server Name

The server name is the domain name that the Apache server will be serving files to. You may specify a domain name or an IP address as the server name attribute, but in this case, you would enter the local loopback address:

ServerName 127.0.0.1

The ServerName directive tells the Apache server what the URL of the server is to be. If you are using Apache as a developer server on your own desktop computer, use a server name of "127.0.0.1." This is the local loopback address and will allow you to serve pages on your own machine from your own machine.

# Setting the Document Root

The document root is the location of the directory that will be serving the pages for your website. It is given as a file system location. The following example is a document root as given on a Windows machine:

```
DocumentRoot "C:\Apache\htdocs"
```

The DocumentRoot directive tells the server where to find the HTML files that will be served and is a reflection of your file system. It is also used to show the general location of the CGI-BIN for Perl scripts.

# Setting the CGI-BIN Location

In order to use Perl with your Apache installation, Perl will have to be installed on the local machine. The CGI-BIN location shows the location of the Perl scripts that your Apache server will be serving:

```
ScriptAlias /cgi-bin/ "C:\apache\htdocs\cgi-bin\"
```

The example sets the ScriptAlias location. This tells the server where to expect CGI scripts. Your ScriptAlias doesn't need to be within the document or server root – you can have it anywhere on the local machine, on any operating system supported.

You may specify the location and name of your CGI-BIN as something other than the norm. Apache has provided this functionality for those server setups that don't conform to the norm. Using a setup in this manner isn't the norm but can be a fun way to personalize your website to your specifications. You don't even have to have your CGI scripts end with the .cgi or .pl extension. You can use something descriptive to conform to your site's theme. Simply use the knowledge in the coming pages to change the Apache directives to conform to your theme.

What you would do is alter the default settings within your httpd.conf file, which is the main configuration file that Apache uses at startup to apply the settings that you have chosen. These settings don't have to include the default settings – you may specify anything you like. There are several large sites that I've encountered that use a custom setup such as this. They've used the theme of their site to their advantage, adding a customized flair to their configuration files that are reflected in the address bar in the browser.

# Summary

In this chapter, we learned about the Apache web server. Apache is a great server to work with, as we touched on. It's a powerful and capable server that offers many configuration options. Every option and all functionality possibilities of the Apache are beyond the scope of this book – it is a book unto itself.

# CHAPTER 10

# Scripted Email: Using sendmail

This chapter will cover sendmail, a widely known Linux daemon that enables you to schedule and send a larger number of emails. I'll show you how to do this quickly and easily using Perl scripts, with values taken from a database.

## Setting the Stage

To start, we must lay the ground work, starting with some simple HTML markup. The HTML code to allow a FORM control to upload an image is simple but very important in its constituent parts. The HTML markup that we'll use for this section's discussion is given in Listing 10-1.

***Listing 10-1.*** The HTML markup

```
<table border="0" align="center">
<tr>
      <form name="form1" method="post" action="upload.pl"
      enctype="multipart/form-data">
      <td align="center" valign="top"> 1.<input type="file" name="FILE0">
      </input></td>
</tr><tr>
      <td align="center" valign="top"> 2.<input type="file" name="FILE1">
      </input></td>
</tr><tr>
      <td align="center" valign="top"> 3.<input type="file" name="FILE2">
      </input></td>
```

161

T. Valentine, *Database-Driven Web Development*, https://doi.org/10.1007/978-1-4842-9792-6_10

```
</tr><tr>
    <td align="center" valign="top" input type="submit" value="Upload
    Image(s)"></td>
    </form>
</tr>
</table>
```

As you can see, there are three file fields being displayed. Each one has a name attribute that is unique and is listed in a logical order. The input type of "file" tells the browser to expect a file upload of some kind. The enctype="multipart/form-data" is essential to the success of the upload and cannot be left out. The name of the file and then the data (the file's contents) are sent to the server in two completely separate parts. Because of this, it is said to be a multipart form.

The simple HTML I used for the example really is all it takes to make an aesthetically pleasing page element. Now let's get into the upload script itself. As with all Perl scripts, the script starts on its first line, an area called the shebang. Linux servers are the norm on the Web, so the path to find Perl.exe is usually #!/usr/bin/perl.

The path may be anything, really, but it's always good to stay with normal conventions and protocols when describing the path to an object. On a Windows computer, the shebang is usually as shown in Listing 10-2.

*Listing 10-2.* The shebang on a Windows workstation

```
C:\Progra~@\Perl\bin\perl
```

The first chunk of Perl script to be addressed is as shown in Listing 10-3.

*Listing 10-3.* Required param() and upload() code snippets

```
$thisfilename0 = $cgi->param('FILE0');
$thisfilename1 = $cgi->param('FILE1');
$thisfilename2 = $cgi->param('FILE2');
$thisfile0 = $cgi->upload('FILE0');
$thisfile1 = $cgi->upload('FILE1');
$thisfile2 = $cgi->upload('FILE2');
```

As always, there are considerations that much be addressed while designing your scripts. I've found that processing the parameters and script's data at the top of the script worked the best, as Perl reads and executes from the top down. I have also found that keeping the script as simple as possible is always the best way to go. You can see that the variables are all uniquely identified.

The very first mistake a developer will make when starting to write their first uploader is to only use a param() method to catch the data or only an upload() method to catch the data. The fact is you have to use both methods, as  you can see in the preceding block of code. Use the param() method to handle the file name. The data within the file is transported using the upload() method.

This is where it gets interesting. We're working with files and Perl modules in this section, so let's start with why I started a file manipulation with the use of a length() method. The reason I weigh the variable is to check if an HTML input field was left empty. There are three file locations to upload with. I simply weigh the variable to see if the input field was left empty. If it's empty, @thumb and @thesefiles will not have data pushed onto them. This has connotations for the code given in Listing 10-4.

***Listing 10-4.*** Weighing the size of a piece of data and acting upon it

```
$thisLength0 = length($thisfilename0);
if ($thisLength0 > 0) {
      open(FILE0, ">/$dirPath/$thisfilename0;
      while(<$thisfile0>) {
      print FILE0;
      };
      close FILE0;
      push @thumb, "tn_" . $thisfilename0;
      push @thesefiles, $thisfilename0;
      copy ("/$dirPath/$thisfilename0",  "/$dirPath/tn_$thisfilename0");
};
```

After weighing $thisfilename0, a simple if statement decides if the file is to be created and stored and named. Next comes a while() statement, which is used to read the data in $thisfile0. The print FILE0 statement then writes the data to the file, the name of which is in $thisfilename0. The data stream is then closed.

In order to refer to the proper variable names that hold your data, in particular the file names, I pushed the file name and the thumbnail name onto arrays, @thumb and @thesefiles. A simple concatenation of the original file name indicates that a thumbnail of the uploaded file will be created and called a thumbnail, the name of which starts with "tn_".

```
$count = "0";
foreach (@thesefiles) {

// Resize the full size image in $file, if required. Height has to be over
1500 and width 640
// Get the size of the uploaded file
($globe_x, $globe_y) = imgsize("/$dirPath/$thesefiles[$count]");

//  find out if to resize at all. this is for the resize of the original image
if (($globe_x or $globe_y) > 640) {

// fix x and y divide by zero potential with an if statement
if ($globe_x <= 0) {
     $globe_x = "1";
};
if ($globe_y <= 0) {
     $globe_y = "1";
};

// resize the width to a maximum of 640, proportionally, if required
$ratio = $globe_y / $globe_x;
if ($globe_y > 640) {
     $globe_y = "640";
     $globe_x = $globe_y / $ratio;
}
$newwidth1 = int($globe_y);

// resize the height to a maximum of 1500, proportionally, if required
$ratio = $globe_y / $globe_x;
if ($globe_x >= 1500) {
     $globe_x = "1500";
     $globe_y = $globe_x / $ratio;
}
```

164

```
$newheight1 = int($globe_x);

$image = Image::Magick->new();
$image->Read("/$dirPath/$thesefiles[$count]");
$image->Resize(geometry => "$newheight1x$newwidth1");
$image->Write("/$dirPath/$thesefiles[$count]");
};
```

Next comes the decision on when to resize the image. The first piece of information we'll need to generate is a ratio of $globe_x and $globe_y, which is stated as "$ratio = $globe_y / $globe_x". The size is then tested with an if statement, which, if higher than 640, globe_y becomes 640 and $globe_x becomes the result of the division of $globe_y / $ratio. $newwidth1 becomes the integer value of $globe_x, which is the final value before actually resizing, should the limit of 640 pixels wide be exceeded.

The same set of code that decided if the image was to be resized by exceeding the width is used to calculate the maximum height. Images with a height exceeding 1500 pixels are resized.

Now is when we'll do the actual image manipulation. We'll call on Image::Magick by creating a new Image::Magick object. We will then perform three operations: Read(), Resize(), and Write(), each on their own line.

We start with a $count = "0" declaration. The $count, which is zero based, is fed to a foreach statement. Every time the foreach loop iterates, a 100 × 100 pixel thumbnail is generated, preserving proportions, as in Listing 10-5.

***Listing 10-5.*** The process of uploading, catching, and formatting the data within an mage file

```
### Begin processing the @thumbs
$count = "0";
foreach (@thumb) {
### Begin processing the $thumb, resizing to 100 square
# Get the size of the uploaded file
($globe_x, $globe_y) = imgsize("/home/public_html/content/$thumb[$count]");

### find out if to resize at all. this is for the resize of the
orginial image
### big if statement starts here
```

```
if (($globe_x or $globe_y) > 100) {

### fix x and y divide by zero potential with an if statement each
if ($globe_x <= 0) {
     $globe_x = "1";
};
if ($globe_y <= 0) {
     $globe_y = "1";
};

### resize the width to a maximum of 100, proportionally, if required
$ratio = $globe_y / $globe_x;
if ($globe_y > 100) {
     $globe_y = "100";
     $globe_x = $globe_y / $ratio;
}
$newwidth2 = int($globe_y);

### resize the height to a maximum of 100, proportionally, if required
$ratio = $globe_y / $globe_x;
if ($globe_x > 100) {
     $globe_x = "100";
     $globe_y = $globe_x / $ratio;
}
$newheight2 = int($globe_x);

$image = Image::Magick->new();
$image->Read("/home/public_html/content/$thumb[$count]");
$image->Resize(geometry => "$newheight2 x $newwidth2");
$image->Write("/home/public_html/content/$thumb[$count]");

++$count;
};
```

You can now see how images can be resized via scripted action. Do try to play around with it.

So we're done with manipulating images. Next comes the generation of the HTML markup that will display your uploaded, thumbed images in the browser. Examine the block of code given in Listing 10-6.

**Listing 10-6.** Generating the HTML markup that illustrates the URL of the uploaded file

```
### Begin processing the 3 images uploaded
$count = "0";
$filesuploaded = @thumb;
foreach (@thumb) {

        $onecontentelement = qq{<td align="center" width="100" height="100">
        <img src="http://www.domain.com/content/$thumb[$count]"></td>};

        push @contentarray, $onecontentelement;
        ++$count;
};
```

We first declare $count = "0". We will use this number, incremented after every iteration of the foreach loop, to load values into @contentarray. We build the HTML one step at a time, adding HTML code every time the foreach statement iterates. $onecontentelement contains a TD element, the value of which changes as $count is incremented on the last line of the foreach statement.

You may think that after generating the HTML markup for each thumb we're done with that, but now we have to lay out some rules as to what markup will be encapsulating your generated code. In the following section, we run into some scripting concerns that we have to discuss.

Because Perl is an inline language, the execution starts from the top and goes down. When writing the HTML for your page, you at first have to realize where in the complete document your generated content will be. Peruse the code given in Listing 10-7.

**Listing 10-7.** Showing the process of building and serving the HTML containing database values

```
$topofcontent = qq{HTML>
<HEAD>
<TITLE>EasyUploader.pl</TITLE>
</HEAD>
```

```
<BODY>
<table border="0" cellpadding="0" cellspacing="0" align="center"
valign="top">
<tr>
      <td height="10"></td>
</tr><tr>
      <td align="center" valign="middle"> Upload Successful!</td>
</tr><tr>
      <td height="10"></td>
</tr><tr>
      <td align="center" valign="middle">$filesuploaded Files Uploaded</td>
</tr><tr>
      <td height="10"></td>
</tr><tr>
      <td align="center" valign="middle">Showing $filesuploaded Thumbs</td>
</tr>};

$bottomofcontent = qq{<tr>
      <td height="10"></td>
</tr>
</table>

</BODY>
</HTML>};

### print da page
print qq{Content-type: text/html\n\n};
print qq{$topofcontent @contentarray $bottomofcontent};
```

Alright, so we've discussed an upload script, but we're not entirely completed. You must give thought to how you're going to get the script to print your formatted HTML markup to the browser. As you can see in the preceding block of code, there are two print commands. The first is used to tell the browser what type of data to expect, in this case "text/html".

Then comes another print command, this time stating that $topofcontent @content and $bottomofcontent be printed, in that order. If you look, you'll see that the top of a table is in $topofcontent and the bottom of a table is in $bottomofcontent.

We put @content in the middle because the HTML will be sent in exactly that order: the content generated on the fly and stuffed into @content is printed in the right order, in this case showing up to three image thumbnails.

# Summary

In this chapter, we examined a really cool solution to quickly and easily send out an email blast using only a handful of Perl scripts, with values selected from a database. Flat files were also used as the source of a static page of data. sendmail is a universally known Linux daemon that allows you to send millions of emails a day, should you want to.

# CHAPTER 11

# A Database-Driven Menu System

So we've all seen drop-down menus on great sites. They're a timeless feature – they've been used for decades and will no doubt be used for many more. In this chapter, we'll be using the knowledge presented in an earlier chapter on JavaScript machinations about how HTML, CSS, DOM, and JavaScript work together to provide some pretty amazing functionality. Employ the Perl scripting language and the MySQL database and you've got the makings of a very powerful web page feature.

## How Do Drop-down Menus Work?

Drop-down menus are simple to understand, given a few pointers. Your drop-down menu uses the GET method for loading the links that you'll be using. Values are passed to a script via the parameters stated within the anchor element.

## create.pl

As with most Perl scripts, there are always a few tables that have to be created before the script with the working features is called upon. These scripts are usually for account information like contact information or personal details – names and addresses, for example. The limit to what you can do is governed by your imagination.

create.pl is a simple script that begins our foray into the drop-down menu system. I use it to create the base tables that we'll be working with in a later section of this chapter. We aren't filling in any values in this simple script. We're simply creating the base tables where the values will be stored through the use of other scripts. Examine Listing 11-1.

© Thomas Valentine 2023
T. Valentine, *Database-Driven Web Development*, https://doi.org/10.1007/978-1-4842-9792-6_11

**Listing 11-1.** Examining create.pl

```perl
#!/usr/bin/perl
use DBI;
use CGI;
use CGI::Carp qw(fatalsToBrowser);

$cgi = new CGI;

### connect
$dbh = DBI->connect('DBI:mysql:host=localhost;
database=menu_system', 'user_name', 'password',
{'RaiseError' => 1}) or die "Cannot Connect to Database";

$query = qq{CREATE TABLE pages (
     id INT NOT NULL AUTO_INCREMENT PRIMARY KEY,
     id1 VARCHAR (250) NOT NULL,
     id2 VARCHAR (250) NOT NULL,
     hits VARCHAR (250) NOT NULL
     )};
$sth = $dbh->prepare($query);
$sth->execute();
$sth->finish();
$dbh->disconnect();
### print da shtuff
print qq{Content-type: text/html\n\n};
print qq{<html>
<head>
<title>Create Menu Tables</title>
</head>
<body bgcolor="white">
<table border = "0" cellspacing="0" cellpadding="0" align="center">
<tr>
     <td align="center">Database Tables Created</td>
</table>
</body>
</html>};
1;
```

As you can see, we connect to the database and create a table named "pages." This is an empty table right now, but the next working script will put values in the database, as you'll see soon. This is the first time you'll see the id, id1, id2, and hits columns. I use them with pretty much every project I take on. They're a starting point of the database model. As your project grows, so too will the complexity of your database system.

The first step in this small script is simply the database connection code. It has four items that are used to state where the database is (localhost), what database is being used (database name), a username, and a password.

The database location is stated as localhost. This is used when the Perl script and the MySQL database are running on the same server. If you were using a multiserver setup, you could state a URL or IP address as this value.

The database name is simply what you named the database. It can be any letter or number, but try not to incorporate punctuation into your database names. Some commonly used punctuation can interfere with a script. The left single quote is notorious for this. Depending where and what you're doing with the script, a warning message could be thrown or a fatal error could be thrown. Usernames and passwords should follow this convention as well.

After the database connection code comes the creation of the tables. Note that the id column is auto_increment. This means that the id column will start with a value of zero. This number will be increased by one every time a new table row gets inserted into the database. This is a handy way of specifying the order your table data will be organized within the variables and arrays that will be used to generate the completed document.

The other columns within the table I created are id1, id2, and hits. id1 and id2 can be any type of data you wish. I'm including them here to give you a better understanding of how you should organize your database tables, rows, and columns.

After completing the table creation, I send a small but fully formed HTML document to the browser's target, which is the current browser window. The table is now ready to use.

# populate.pl

The populate.pl script is used to insert values into the database. As I stated before, you want your database tables to be intuitively obvious. There are four columns to the table we'll be using: an auto_increment id, id1, id2, and hits. What we'll be doing with this script is inserting the menu items into a database via variables and arrays.

The menu system we're ultimately building up to consists of two drop-down menus. The first, simply called heading1, consists of two links. The second drop-down menu is entitled heading2 and has four list items. What makes heading2 interesting is that the list items are in two columns. This is a handy feature to know about if you have an inordinately long list of menu items. Breaking one long list into two shorter lists will make the menu easier to read and will be a more obvious and functional page item (Listing 11-2).

**Listing 11-2.** Examining populate.pl

```perl
#!/usr/bin/perl
use DBI;
use CGI;
use CGI::Carp qw(fatalsToBrowser);

$cgi = new CGI;

### create the heading1 and heading2 variables and arrays
@link1 = ('1', '2');
@link2 = ('1', '2', '3', '4');
$id1 = "1";
$id2 = "2";

### connect, damnit !!!
$dbh = DBI->connect('DBI:mysql:host=localhost;database=databasename',
'username', 'password', {'RaiseError' => 1}) or die "Cannot Connect to
Database";
$count = "0";
foreach (@link1) {
    $query = qq{INSERT INTO pages (id1, id2)
        VALUES
    ('$id1', '$link1[$count]')};
    $sth = $dbh->prepare($query);
    $sth->execute;
    ++$count;
};
```

```perl
$count = "0";
foreach (@link2) {
     $query = qq{INSERT INTO pages (id1, id2)
          VALUES
     ('$id2', '$link2[$count]')};
     $sth = $dbh->prepare($query);
     $sth->execute;
     ++$count;
};
$sth->finish();
$dbh->disconnect();
### print da schtuff
print qq{Content-type: text/html\n\n};
print qq{<html>
<head>
<title>Experiment</title>
</head>
<body bgcolor="white">
<table border = "0" cellspacing="0" cellpadding="0" align="center">
<tr>
     <td align="center">Database Entries Inserted</td>
</table>
</body>
</html>};
1;
```

As you can see, populate.pl is a good example of the beginnings of a really great menu system. The two arrays are looped through and stuffed into the database along with the two $id1 and $id2 variables.

After the minor database insertions, some HTML markup was sent to the browser, showing a small message that everything went well.

# page.cgi

As with all Perl scripts, we start with the shebang. I always declare the modules to be used at the top of the script. This makes it easy to see at a glance what modules the script is using. There are two parameters being passed to the script: id1 and id2. They are contained within the intuitively named $id1 and $id2 variables. page.cgi shows the ease with which values can be passed to a script. It also shows where to fit in your database calls and the generation of HTML content.

Examine Listing 11-3, which is a complete script that stores the id1 and id2 parameters in a table named pages. Notice also that there is a "hits" column. This is incremented every time the script is run with its own very simple statement.

***Listing 11-3.*** Examining page.cgi

```
#!/usr/bin/perl
use DBI;
use CGI;
use CGI::Carp qw(fatalsToBrowser);

$cgi = new CGI;

$id1 = $cgi->param('id1');
$id2 = $cgi->param('id2');

### connect, damnit !!!
$dbh = DBI->connect('DBI:mysql:host=localhost;
database=menu_system', 'user_name', 'password', {'RaiseError' => 1})
or die "Cannot Connect to Database";

$query = qq{INSERT INTO pages (id1, id2) VALUES ('$id1', '$id2') WHERE id2
= $id2};
$sth = $dbh->prepare($query);
$sth->execute;
$query = qq{UPDATE pages SET Hits = Hits + 1 WHERE id2 = $id2};
$sth = $dbh->prepare($query);
$sth->execute;
$query = qq{SELECT id1, id2, hits FROM pages WHERE id2 = $id2};
$sth = $dbh->prepare($query);
```

```
$sth->execute();
while (@thisid = $sth->fetchrow_array()) {
      $id1 = $thisid[0];
      $id2 = $thisid[1];
      $hits = $thisid[2];
}
$sth->finish();
$dbh->disconnect();
### print da shtuff
print qq{Content-type: text/html\n\n};
print qq{<html>
<head>
<title>Experiment</title>
</head>
<body bgcolor="white">
<table border = "0" cellspacing="0" cellpadding="0" align="center">
<tr>
      <td align="center" valign="top">Heading $id1, Page $id2, Visited
      $hits times</td>
</table>
</body>
</html>};
```

We start the database calls with an insertion. The values contained within the id1 and id2 parameters are inserted into the pages table.

# menu.html

Now comes the code to present the document we'll be working with. I've kept the HTML markup as simple as possible to aid in learning. Most of you should be able to make sense of the simple but fully formed web page that is given as the next topic of discussion.

# Code Block One

This block of code represents an entire selection of CSS rules. As always, I've kept it to a minimum of code to aid in learning. Notice that we started with a simple <html> element at the top of the page. The !DOCTYPE element is no longer required.

The CSS rules in this list show seven styles. Get used to using CSS rules in the head of the document. Note that CSS rules are within opening and closing braces and are encapsulated in their entirety within the opening and closing <STYLE> elements.

```
<html>
<head>
<title>--- Menu System ---</title>
<style>
body{font-family:arial;}
table{font-size:10pt;
    background:#336699;
}
a{
    color:white;
    text-decoration:none;
    font:bold;
}
a:hover{
    color:white;
    text-decoration: underline;
}
td.menu{
    background:#336699;
}
table.menu {
    font-size:10pt;
    position:absolute;
    visibility:hidden;
}
```

```
.white {
    font-size:10pt;
    color: white;
    font-weight: bold;
}
</style>
```

As you can see, there are a few different syntax combinations that allow CSS to do some pretty powerful operations. td.menu applies to all TD elements with the name attribute of "menu." The same goes with table.menu.

## Begin Code Block Two

This simple but essential block of code is where we'll start getting into the functionality of the database-driven drop-down menu system we'll be exploring. As always, JavaScript code is stated between the opening and closing <script> elements. You may state your JavaScript code anywhere on the page, but the normal convention is to declare them in the head of the document.

*Listing 11-4.* Syntax of a getElementById() statement

```
<script type="text/javascript">
function showmenu(elmnt) {
    document.getElementById(elmnt).style.visibility="visible";
}
function hidemenu(elmnt) {
    document.getElementById(elmnt).style.visibility="hidden";
}
</script>
</head>
```

This block of code, Listing 11-4, switches the visibility() to visible or hidden. The reason we do this here is because we want the entire document to have the option of employing a drop-down menu. It's always a good idea to insert your JavaScript in the head of the document, every time.

# Code Block Three

Now comes the BODY of the document. The HTML markup we're exploring is simple and intuitive even if you only have a glimmer of what is entailed in writing document content. We begin with a simple table declaration that shows the basic dimensions of the table followed by further table data, utilized by TR and TD elements. Note that the bottommost block of markup shows two columns, side by side. This will translate into a multicolumn menu when the visible() method is toggled.

```html
<html>
<body>
<table border="0" cellpadding="0" cellspacing="0" align="center"
width="400">
<tr bgcolor="#336699">
    <td height="20" align="left"
    onmouseover="showmenu('menu1')"
    onmouseout="hidemenu('menu1')" class="white">  Heading 01
    <table border="0" cellpadding="5" cellspacing="0" align="center"
    class="menu" id="menu1">
    <tr>
        <td width="150" class="menu"><a href="page.cgi?id1=1&id2=1"
        onmouseover="showmenu('menu1')"
        onmouseout="hidemenu('menu1')"
        target="output">List Item</a>
        </td>
    </tr><tr>
        <td width="150" class="menu"><a href="page.cgi?id1=1&id2=2"
        onmouseover="showmenu('menu1')"
        onmouseout="hidemenu('menu1')"
        target="output">List Item</a>
        </td>
    </tr>
    </table>
    </td>
```

```
<td height="20" align="right"
onmouseover="showmenu('menu2')"
onmouseout="hidemenu('menu2')" class="white">Heading 02  
<table border="0" cellpadding="5" cellspacing="0" align="center"
class="menu" id="menu2" width="175">
<tr>
        <td width="150" class="menu"><a href="page.cgi?id1=2&id2=5"
        onmouseover="showmenu('menu2')"
        onmouseout="hidemenu('menu2')"
        target="output">List Item</a>
        </td>
        <td width="150" class="menu"><a href="page.cgi?id1=2&id2=6"
        onmouseover="showmenu('menu2')"
        onmouseout="hidemenu('menu2')"
        target="output">List Item</a>
        </td>
</tr><tr>
        <td width="150" class="menu"><a href="page.cgi?id1=2&id2=7"
        onmouseover="showmenu('menu2')"
        onmouseout="hidemenu('menu2')"
        target="output">List Item</a>
        </td>
        <td width="150" class="menu"><a href="page.cgi?id1=2&id2=8"
        onmouseover="showmenu('menu2')"
        onmouseout="hidemenu('menu2')"
        target="output">List Item</a>
        </td>
</tr>
</table>
</td>
</tr>
</table>
</body>
</html>
```

Take note of how the menu data is placed in the document. You can have as many drop-down menu windows as you can fit on a page. Of particular import are the id and name attributes. They are stated in multiple locations to ensure the menu data is displayed in the right menu.

## Begin Code Block Four

Block four consists of the declaration of a simple table that encapsulates an iFrame. As you might have noticed in an earlier code example, all of the anchor elements had the target attribute set to "output." The iFrame is designated as "output" via the name attribute. Because of this, the output of the scripts will be written to the iFrame. The entire page won't refresh, only the contents of the iFrame. All of the scripts in this chapter are put together in this way so all output is written to the iFrame.

```
<html>
<body>
<table border="0" cellpadding="0" cellspacing="0" align="center">
<tr>
      <td height="50"></td>
</tr>
</table>
<table border="0" cellpadding="0" cellspacing="0" align="center">
<tr>
      <td align="center">
<iframe name="output" src="empty.html"
cols="50" rows="30">
</iframe>
      </td>
</tr>
</table>
</body>
</html>
```

As you can see, the file named empty.html is first loaded into the iFrame window. This could just as easily have been a fully formed Perl script that is able to perform database interactions and then write the generated content to the iFrame.

# Summary

In this chapter, we explored the creation of a simple but functional database-driven drop-down menu system. Drop-down menu systems are here to stay. Now you know how to create a basic drop-down menu, but you can also play around with it and add features.

# APPENDIX A

# From Flat File to Database

I was once tasked to come up with a solution to a web developer's problem. She needed some 1200 HTML files put into a database, stripping the HTML markup and leaving behind only text files. She stripped the HTML code with a Regular Expression I gave her. It was the text files, formerly HTML documents, that needed to be put into the database.

We decided to put the HTML files into a database because handling 1200 HTML files was becoming cumbersome. Placing the informative text within a database to be served using just a few scripts was a better method of delivering the information to the user. Using a database-driven solution such as this also makes edits easy, with just a few more Perl scripts used to edit the information.

I decided that each line of each file should be a table row, with the contents of each file being a table. I used the name of the file for the table name and added that name to a lookup table for easy access later on.

The beauty and flexibility of Perl are demonstrated very well in this small construction. The entire process took under two minutes to perform on our little testing server and resulted in a database that is easily referenced due to the simplicity of the database model.

By nesting three foreach loops, I was able to perform the step-by-step operation with a minimum of fuss, cycling first through @dirlist for the directory names, then through @filelist for each file, which was then opened and read. The file data was split on the new lines and placed into the @split_text array. For each $filename[$filename_count], we added a table and populated it if the if statement evaluated to true. This is what I came up with:

```perl
#!/usr/bin/perl

use CGI;
use DBI;
use CGI::Carp (fatalsToBrowser);
```

© Thomas Valentine 2023
T. Valentine, *Database-Driven Web Development*, https://doi.org/10.1007/978-1-4842-9792-6

```perl
$cgi = new CGI;

### make the directory list
@dirlist = (DirList0, DirList1, DirList2, DirList3, DirList4, DirList5,
DirList6, DirList7, DirList8, DirList9, DirList10, DirList11, DirList12,
DirList13, DirList14, DirList15, DirList16, DirList17, DirList18,
DirList19);

### connect to the database
$dsn = "DBI:mysql:database=database_name;host=localhost";
$user = "username";
$password = "password";
$dbh = DBI->connect($dsn, $user, $password, {RaiseError => 1,
AutoCommit => 0});
### create the master table
$query = qq{CREATE TABLE master (
            id INT NOT NULL AUTO_INCREMENT PRIMARY KEY,
            tablename VARCHAR (200) NOT NULL,
            category VARCHAR (200)
            )};
$sth = $dbh->prepare($query);
$sth->execute();

$count = "0";
$dirlist_count = "0";
$filelist_count = "0";
$type = "text";
foreach (@dirlist) {
     while ($thisfile = <$dirlist[$dirlist_count]/*.txt>) {
          push @filelist, $thisfile;
     }
     foreach (@filelist) {
          open (FILEHANDLE, "$dirlist[$dirlist_
          count]/$filelist[$filelist_count]");
          $text = "";
          $newtext = "";
```

```
while (read (FILEHANDLE, $newtext, 1)) {
      $text .= $newtext;
}
close FILEHANDLE;
@split_text = split "\n", $text;
$split_text_count = "0";
foreach (@split_text) {
      $split_text[$split_text_count] =~ s/\n+//g;
      $this_split = $split_text[$split_text_count];
      $this_split =~ s/[ ]+//g;
      if ($this_split != "") {
            $query = qq{CREATE TABLE $filelist[$filelist_
            count] (
                  type VARCHAR (200) NOT NULL,
                  text BLOB
                  )};
            $sth = $dbh->prepare($query);
            $sth->execute();
            $query = qq{INSERT INTO $filelist[$filelist_
            count] (
                  type,
                  text
                  ) VALUES (
                  '$type',
                  '$split_text[$split_text_count]'
                  )};
            $sth = $dbh->prepare($query);
            $sth->execute();
            $query = qq{INSERT INTO master (
                  tablename,
                  category
                  ) VALUES (
                  '$filelist[$filelist_count]',
                  '$dirlist[$dirlist[$count]'
                  )};
```

```
                           $sth = $dbh->prepare($query);
                           $sth->execute();
                           ++$split_text_count;
                           ++$count;
                }
          ++$filelist_count;
          }
      ++$dirlist_count;
      }
### print da shtuff
print qq{Content-type: text/html\n\n};
print qq{I'm Done!<br>};
print qq{I have created $count tables};
exit;
```

The @dirlist array holds the names of the directories the files are placed in, and each file within the directory is glob'd for the file names that are placed in @filelist. I then used a foreach loop to open and read each file byte by byte, the contents of which are placed in the aptly named scalar $text.

I then split $text on the new lines and added each new line of text into @split_text. I removed the new line characters and proceeded to make a copy of each item within $this_split to later test if there is no data in the array item, as each original text file had several blank lines. We split on the new line characters and then removed them, remember, so each file will have empty items (file rows) in @split_text that we don't want to see as part of the database.

I removed every space from the copied array item. If the copied array item was empty, the script would not do anything but continue on to the next item in @split_text through the use of the aforementioned foreach loop.

If $this_split != "" evaluated to true, I then created a table using the file name as the table name and populated it with rows, each row of the text file being worked on being a row in the table. Each table name was then placed in the master lookup table.

# APPENDIX B

# Internet Socket Programming Using Perl

The role of Perl on the Internet is hard to ignore. Some would make the case that Perl is the most used and most capable scripting language on the Internet today, and this is probably true. Its versatility and ease of use have made it an industry standard, used throughout the world.

Perl sockets work like file handles that can span across a network or the entire Internet. With sockets, you may communicate with any computer that is connected via the Internet or via a network. To communicate with this other computer, you specify the server to connect to and a port to connect through. After the initial connection, you may use that connection just as you would a file handle. There are a few differences, but these are mainly academic.

To put it simply, the two sides of a Perl socket are the server and the client. It doesn't really matter which is which – the communication process is essentially the same, as the client can send information to the server, and vice versa. The communication process is surprisingly simple. The process starts with the creation of the server. The server patiently waits for a connection request from the client, which can be created any time after the creation of the server. The client connects to the server using the address of the server and the mutually agreed-upon port number. If the port numbers are different, no connection is made. Once the client is connected, data may be sent from the server to the client, and vice versa.

Now there are two ways that data may be sent over a socket: both ways using one socket, or one-way using two sockets. In the one-socket method, data is sent from the server to the client and from the client to the server using one socket for both. In the two-socket method, one socket is used to send data from the server to the client and one is used to send data from the client to the server. We'll be touching on both methods in this appendix, so read on.

189

© Thomas Valentine 2023
T. Valentine, *Database-Driven Web Development*, https://doi.org/10.1007/978-1-4842-9792-6

Sockets exist on all major operating systems. They are the accepted way to achieve communication between computers. Keeping this in mind, you may connect a UNIX computer to a Windows computer (and vice versa) with little or no troubles – if Perl is successfully installed on both machines. It should be noted that the ports used for an operation like this differ from OS to OS. Just keep in mind a few simple facts: ports below 1024 are normally reserved for system use, so save yourself a headache and don't use them. HTTP requests usually use port 80, for example. Using a port number roughly in the 1025 to 5000 range usually produces adequate results. Just be sure to use the same port on both computers being connected. Now, let's get on to the practical coding.

Before you can connect to a server, or even create the server, you must know whether you can establish a connection on that port. To do this, use the can_read or can_write method of the IO::Select module, which is included with Perl. The following example checks four sockets to see which ones are available for the connection:

```
Use IO::Select

$select = IO::Select->new();

$select->add($socket1);
$select->add($socket2);
$select->add($socket3);
$select->add($socket4);

@ok_to_read = $select->can_read($timeout);

foreach $socket (@ok_to_read) {
        $socket->recv($data_buffer, $flags)
        print $data_buffer;
        }
```

This example uses the can_read method to check if any of the sockets may be used. You can just as easily use the can_write method in this particular example – the end result is the same. The script starts with the declaration of the use of the IO::Select module. A new instance named $select is then created, using the new() method. Four sockets are then created using the add() method. The sockets are then placed into the @ok_to_read array, where the can_read method is invoked. A foreach loop is then used to print the results from the can_read call to the contents of the @ok_to_read array. The recv method is used to send info through the socket. Using the recv or send functions, you can send byte streams through your socket. You can also use the simple print and angle operators (< and >) to send text through the socket. Just be sure to use the newline character (\n) at the end of each line if it's text you're sending. The newline character is required to send the text string through the socket – if there is no newline character, no data is sent.

Now that you know how to check the sockets, we can delve into the creation of the common servers and clients that Perl is able to use. We'll start with the creation of a TCP server and a TCP client using IO::Socket. Since both the server and the client work hand in hand, we'll cover them both at the same time. There are, however, a few bases that we have to cover, namely, the parameters that are passed to the new() method of IO::Socket::INET. There are eight of them, listed as follows:

1. PeerAddr – Is the DNS address of the machine you'd like to connect to. The address may be the dotted IP address of the machine or the domain name itself – "walkthegeek.com", for example.

2. PeerPort – Is the port on the host machine you'd like to connect to. We'll use port 2000, for no particular reason.

3. Proto – Is the protocol that will be used, the options being tcp or udp.

4. Type – Is the type of connection you'd like to establish, the options being SOCK_STREAM for tcp data, SOCK_DGRAM for udp connections, or SOCK_SEQPACKET for sequential data packet connections. We'll be using tcp, so the SOCK_STREAM connection type will be used.

5. LocalAddr – Is the local address to be bound, if there is one. We won't use one.

6. LocalPort – Is the local port number to be used.

7. Listen – Is the queue size, which is the maximum number of connections allowed.

8. Timeout – Is the timeout value for connections.

All socket communications using IO::Socket use these same parameters. We'll use the new() method of IO::Socket::INET to return a scalar, which holds a file handle, which is an indirect file handle type. Let's make a client, as seen here:

```
use IO::Socket

$socket = IO::Socket::INET->new
        (
        PeerAddr => 'walkthegeek.com',
        PeerPort => '2000',
        Proto => 'tcp',
        Type = 'SOCK_STREAM'
        ) or die "Could not Open Port.\n";
```

So there you go. You've made a TCP client using the sockets of IO::Socket::INET. It really is that easy. Now let's write to the server from the client. The connection coding is the same, so it doesn't need to be repeated. As in the example shown previously, the port used is 2000, the server is walkthegeek.com, the protocol is tcp, and the type is SOCK_STREAM.

```
print $socket "Hello there!!\n";

close ($socket);
```

The example sends a text message to the server. The message "Hello there!!" will be displayed on the server's console. Notice that the newline character (\n) has been dutifully used on the end of the print statement. Because we're writing text through the socket, the text will not be transmitted if the newline is omitted.

So that's writing to the server; let's cover reading from the server. The creation of the socket and the subsequent connection is the same; only the print statement changes, as seen here:

```
$answer = <$socket>;

print $answer;

close ($socket);
```

The preceding code pulls the message from the server, displaying it on the console of the client. Creating a server is as easy as creating the client. The same connection coding is used; only the $socket is replaced with $server, as seen here:

```
$server = IO::Socket::INET->new
        (
        PeerAddr => 'walkthegeek.com',
        PeerPort => '2000',
        Proto => 'tcp',
        Type = 'SOCK_STREAM'
        ) or die "Could not Open Port.\n";
```

What changes from the creation of the client to the creation of the server is the coding below the connection snippet – a while loop is used. The following example shows the server reading from the client:

```
while ($client = $server->accept())
{
        $line = <$client>;
        print $line;
        }

close ($server);
```

The while loop calls the accept() method, which makes the server wait for a client to connect. The body of the while loop is executed when the client connects, reading (pulling) any messages from the client.

So that's reading from the client; now let's cover writing to the client. The only thing that changes is the body of the while loop, as seen here:

```
while ($client = $server->accept())
{
        print "Hello Client !!\n";
        }

close ($server);
```

Don't forget the newline character "\n". Omitting it will cause problems, remember. In the examples so far, I've used tcp for the sockets. You can just as easily use udp, however. Just substitute udp for tcp in the Proto parameter, and use SOCK_DGRAM in place of SOCK_STREAM for the Type parameter. Simple.

So you're now at the forefront of Internet Socket programming. With this knowledge, you can create chat programs, run a multiplayer game over the Internet, and just generally have fun.

# APPENDIX C

# Interprocess Communication Essentials

Let's take a look at interprocess communication. Anyone who has had a fairly complex script to churn out has had to deal with this at one time or another. In this document, we'll show the use and structure that is interprocess communication. We'll read and write from parent to child processes, from child to parent processes, and we'll use bidirectional communication to achieve both at the same time.

A process is a task given to the operating system that has its own execution resources, including its own allocation of CPU time. A process may interact with other processes in a number of different ways. We'll explore those ways in this chapter.

The support for interprocess communication with Perl is considerable. At its most basic is the use of backticks to perform system commands such as deleting and copying. When you utilize backticks, as you submit the command, a new child process is created. When the task the child process has been given is complete, the child process reports back to the parent process and the parent script continues.

Perl supplies the fork function to start a new process after setting up a pipe with the pipe command. You may use the open function in lieu of the pipe function, but I'll stick to piping at first.

It should be noted that the use of fork is entirely operating system dependent. It is readily available on Unix or Linux machines, but you'll run into problems on an MS-DOS system as the command is not supported on that platform. On a Windows machine, you may use Object Linking & Embedding (OLE) to send data between processes.

195

© Thomas Valentine 2023
T. Valentine, *Database-Driven Web Development*, https://doi.org/10.1007/978-1-4842-9792-6

On Linux, processes may communicate with each other using signals. Perl implements an easy mechanism for catching signals sent to your processes. All you do is connect a signal handling subroutine to the signal's entry in a predefined %SIG hash. First, we'll set up a machination to catch an INT signal.

```
$SIG{INT} = \&handler_sub;
```

Note that a hard reference to the handler_sub subroutine was used. You may also use symbolic references if required. The handler_sub subroutine simply gets the name of the signal passed as an argument, as seen below:

```
sub handler_sub {
        $forced_scalar = shift;
        die "The signal was $forced_scalar";
}
```

Using a signal handler like this gives you an idea of the ease of use given by Perl for interprocess communication. The die and print make for a clean exit from the subroutine.

It should be noted here that Perl is currently not re-entrant. When a function is re-entrant, you may interrupt processing while still inside the function. You may call it again at any time required because the original state of the data is stored and is restored when the second call to the function exits. If a function is not re-entrant, if you interrupt and call it again, the original data will be overwritten.

Another easy way to play with processes is with the exec function. The exec function executes your commands and doesn't return if the command is executed without error. The exec function will fail and return a false value if the program you call isn't found, for example. That is, exec returns only when an error is encountered. This is the only time that exec will return a value. If you'd like a returned value, you would use system instead of exec. We'll explore system thoroughly in a few paragraphs.

You may pass parameters to exec if required. The way exec treats its parameters is very interesting. The list of parameters passed to exec is parsed, and the first element in the list is treated as the program to run. The next value is a function of the program being executed. That is, if you were to use the copy command, you would specify in the parameters passed to exec the file name to be copied. The first element of the array passed below will be the program to run, and the next item within the array would be the file name.

```
@thisarray = ("copy", "thisfile.txt");

if (exec(@thisarray)) {
        if ($?) {
                die qq{Error Encountered: $?};
        } else {
                die qq{One File Copied. File Name Is: $thisarray[1]};
        }
}
```

I loaded @thisarray with the command and the file name. The exec is executed if @thisarray exists, and the two parameters within @thisarray are used to perform the copy system command.

If no errors are encountered, the program prints and exits. The program also reports if there has been an error placed in $?, which then prints an error message and exits the program without the file being copied.

This simple and intuitive way of creating processes isn't all that is available. To really get an idea of how to use processes, we must explore the system function. When you call a program with exec, the exec function replaces the current program with the one called by exec. If we were to use the system command, however, we'd end up with a program that forks and creates a child process. The program is then executed, and any values you have need for can be returned to the parent.

The means to send data to and from different processes is also a needfully simple task. In the following example, I'll open a program with a pipe, as such:

```
open(THISFILEHANDLE, "thisfile.cgi |");
```

The | character sets the file to pipe its output to the calling program. To make the operation go the other way and send data to the program, simply move the pipe, as such:

```
open(THISFILEHANDLE, "| thisfile.cgi");
```

The child process, then, may be piped to or from depending on what is required. Pipes are fundamental to interprocess communication. The entire read operation would be as follows:

```
open(THISFILEHANDLE, "thisfile.cgi |";

while (<THISFILEHANDLE>) {
        print;
}

close(THISFILEHANDLE);
```

where the file that is opened and executed simply has a print statement in it. This ease of use for reading and writing to different processes is a big reason why Perl has stayed alive all these years. To send data would be just a little different, as such:

```
open(THISFILEHANDLE, "| thisfile.cgi";

print THISFILEHANDLE "Hey There!";

close(THISFILEHANDLE);
```

The example sends the string "Hey There!" to the program that was opened. What the program that was opened does with the string is entirely up to you.

We used named pipes and file handles in the aforementioned examples. Now let's explore STDOUT and STDERR. When you use one of the various interprocess communication methods, the list passed will be parsed for Unix metacharacters. You can use metacharacters to redirect standard file handles such as the aforementioned STDOUT and STDERR.

To redirect a standard file handle, you would refer to them using the Unix file descriptors. STDIN's file descriptor is 0, STDOUT's is 1, and STDERR's is 2. You may use notation such as 1>thisfilename to send STDOUT to a file or you can use the following notation to catch a program's STDOUT and STDERR:

```
$this_value = `this_program 1>&2`;
```

The preceding example shows the backtick method. The open function may also be used to acquire the same result, as shown here:

```
open(THISPIPEHANDLE, "this_program 1>&2 |") or die "Could Not Open Pipe";

while (<THISPIPEHANDLE>) {
        print;
}
```

where this_program has a simple print statement in it. You can see at a glance the amazing flexibility given to you by Perl. You may also write to a child process using the open function, as shown here:

```
if (open(THISCHILDHANDLE, "|-")) {
        print THISCHILDHANDLE "This is a text message";
        close (THISCHILDHANDLE);
}
```

The open statement is used to create a child process of the current process and read from that process by using the "|-" after the process name. The statement creates a new process in THISCHILDHANDLE and causes the program to fork. The statements return false in the child process, and the process is destroyed with the close function.

In the next example, I'll be reading and writing to a child process created with fork using the pipe function and a couple of functions from IO::Handle.

```
Use IO::Handle;

pipe(READHANDLE, WRITEHANDLE);

WRITEHANDLE->autoflush(1);
READHANDLE->autoflush(1);

if ($processed = fork) {
        close(READHANDLE);
        print WRITEHANDLE "Here is some text";
        close(WRITEHANDLE);
        waitpid($processed, 0);
} else {
        close(WRITEHANDLE);
        while (defined($text = <READHANDLE>)) {
                print $text;
        };
        exit;
}
```

We used the autoflush() function of IO::Handle to make sure the pipe is unbuffered. You want it to be unbuffered so the data flows through rather than getting stuck in the pipe. We also used the waitpid() function to wait for the child process to terminate.

You can also write to a parent process from a child process using the open function and a pipe, as shown here:

```
if (open(THISCHILDHANDLE, "-|")) {
        print <THISCHILDHANDLE>;
        close(THISCHILDHANDLE);
} else {
        print "This is a text message";
        exit;
}
```

The preceding example prints "This is a text message" to the parent process from the child process. You can also write to a parent process from a child process if you create a new process with fork, as shown here:

```
Use IO::Handle;

pipe(THISREADHANDLE, THISWRITEHANDLE);

THISWRITEHANDLE->autoflush(1);
THISREADHANDLE->autoflush(1);

if ($processed = fork) {
        close THISWRITEHANDLE;
        while (defined($text = <THISREADHANDLE>)) {
                print $text;
        }
        close THISREADHANDLE;
        waitpid($processed, 0);
} else {
        close THISREADHANDLE;
        print THISWRITEHANDLE "This is a text message";
        exit;
}
```

So that's a lot of interprocess communications to mull over. We'll now get a little more complicated by discussing the use of bidirectional communication. We'll use two pipes to communicate with the processes we'll be creating. We'll write both ways and then kill everything, leaving no lingering processes, as such.

```perl
Use IO:Handle;

pipe(READFROMCHILD, WRITETOPARENT);
pipe(READFROMPARENT, WRITETOCHILD);

READFROMCHILD->autoflush(1);
READFROMPARENT->autoflsuh(1);
WRITETOCHILD->autoflush(1);
WRITETOPARENT->autoflush(1);

if ($this = fork) {
        close READFROMPARENT;
        close WRITETOPARENT;
        print WRITETOCHILD "The parent process says hello";
        $thisdata = <READFROMCHILD>;
        print "The parent process read $thisdata";
        close READFROMCHILD;
        close WRITETOCHILD;
        waitpid(-1, 0);
} else {
        close READFROMCHILD;
        close WRITETOCHILD;
        $thisdata = <READFROMPARENT>;
        print "The child process read $thisdata";
        print WRITETOPARENT "The child process says hello";
        close READFROMPARENT;
        close WRITETOPARENT;
        exit;
}
```

The preceding example is the culmination of everything we've learned so far. We opened two sets of linked pipes, and both wrote and read from one process to another. Using the waitpid(-1, 0) tells waitpid to wait for any process. You can also have waitpid() return a value of 0 immediately if no dead child processes are found, as shown here with the use of POSIX:

```perl
use POSIX "sys_wait_h";
$this_id = waitpid(-1, &WNOHANG);
```

With these handy machinations, you'll be up and running and using processes to get your work done in no time. I hope you enjoyed reading as much as I did writing. Happy programming!

# Index

## A

all[ ], 68, 70
anchors[ ], 68, 70
Apache.exe executable, 156
Apache web server, 137, 142
    administrative access, 150
    C:Apache, 150
    CGI-BIN location, 159
    configuration directives, 158
    DBI.pm, 153–155
    definition, 145
    DNS servers, 149
    downloading/installing binaries,
        146, 147
    function, 145
    handling errors, 145, 146
    httpd.conf file, 156
    installation options, 149
    installation progress window, 152
    operating system, changes, 147–151, 153
    runtime configuration directives,
        158, 159
    ServerName directive, 159
    ServerRoot directive, 158
    stop/restart, 156, 157
    Windows operating system, startup,
        156, 157
applets[ ], 69
ASC/DESC clauses, 44
autoflush() function, 199
AUTO_INCREMENT column, 29
AUTO_INCREMENT id column, 29

## B

Backtick operator, 27, 47, 60
Betas, 130
bgChange() function, 75
BINARY flag, 38
BLOB column types, 33, 38

## C

CGI-BIN location, 159
CGI::Carp module, 21, 55
CGI module, 15, 16
CGI.pm, 16, 20
CGI Primer, 15, 16
CHAR, 38
Character strings, 38
children[ ], 69
classes[ ], 69
@col1, 29, 30, 34
@col2, 29, 30
@col3, 29, 30, 34
Common shebang, 53
Comprehensive Perl Archive Network
    (CPAN), 125, 126
@contentArray, 23, 53–55
content.pl, 22, 23
$count variable, 31
CPAN.bat, 18,
    123, 125, 126
create.pl, 171, 172
CSSproperty, 68
CSS style rules, 66

© Thomas Valentine 2023
T. Valentine, *Database-Driven Web Development*, https://doi.org/10.1007/978-1-4842-9792-6

# D

# E

Printed in the United States
by Baker & Taylor Publisher Services

Printed in the United States
by Baker & Taylor Publisher Services